CORAL REEFS

CITIES UNDER THE SEA

CORAL REEFS

CITIES UNDER THE SEA

Photographs and Text
by
RICHARD C. MURPHY

THE DARWIN PRESS, INC.
PRINCETON, NEW JERSEY

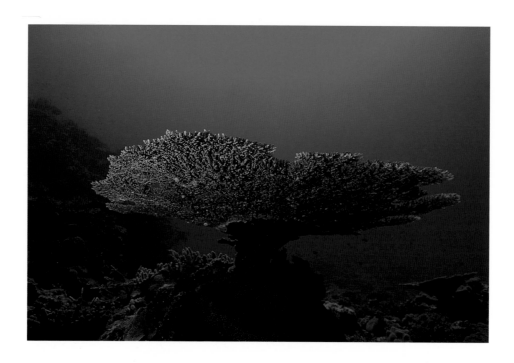

Published by The Darwin Press, Inc. — Second Printing (2007), with revisions
Production and design by John T. Westlake, Darwin Productions

Darwin® Books are printed on acid-free paper and meet the guidelines for
permanence and durability of the Committee on Production Guidelines for Book
Longevity of the Council on Library Resources.♾

Library of Congress Cataloging in Publication Data

Murphy, Richard C., 1942-
    Coral Reefs : cities under the sea / by Richard C. Murphy ; foreword by
      Jean-Michel Cousteau.
         p. cm.
    Included bibliographical references (p.) and index.
ISBN 0-87850-138-X (hardbound)
1.   Coral reef ecology. 2. Coral reefs and islands. I. Title

QH541.5.C7 M87 2002
577.7'89--dc21

                                         2001047719

Printed in China by Regent Publishing Services, Ltd.   www.darwinpress.com

CONTENTS

FOREWORD
by Jean-Michel Cousteau

FOR MOST OF MY LIFE, I have been roaming the sea. Since the age of seven, I have observed the world through a unique window—the faceplate of a dive mask. As the world's first child scuba diver, I experienced the undersea world as a completely alien planet—an intruder among strange and wonderful creatures.

Since those early days, I have had the good fortune of traveling extensively and witnessing first hand many coral reefs around the world. I have seen the vital connections between the health of coral reefs and the quality of people's lives. Today, only half a century after my initial explorations of reefs, I now see reefs under siege from human insult.

Extensive deforestation in Indonesia has released nutrients and sediments that stress reefs. In Papua New Guinea I have seen reefs reduced to rubble from dynamite fishing and local people missing limbs from premature explosions. In Haiti a 10-foot high wall of conch shells, called the pink cliffs, extends along a coastline for almost a mile; the local fishermen now lament the collapse of their fishery and believe the conch population has moved, denying that overharvest is the cause. Although there doesn't seem to be scientific consensus on direct cause and effect to explain the decline in Florida's coral reefs, there are more different diseases affecting a greater number of species over a widening area.

Recent studies suggest that 27 percent of the world's reefs have been destroyed in recent history. Until the last few years it was believed some of the greatest threats were from local activities such as cutting forests, agricultural runoff, pollution, overfishing, and destructive fishing. Unfortunately, a new, more global threat seems to have emerged. It appears that warming of the oceans, which causes

1: Shaded from direct sunlight, soft corals thrive where reef-building corals cannot grow.

7

corals to turn white (bleach) and die, is now having the greatest impact. The El Niño and La Niña events of recent years have killed corals on a global scale and, although some reefs may recover, it is likely that continued warming of the climate will prevent many from restoring themselves. I believe that human use and misuse of energy is contributing to whatever natural climatic changes are taking place. We are undermining the health and vitality of coral reefs on many fronts, both locally and globally. These changes ripple through the oceans and through the entire biosphere. Everything is connected. This fact relates to us and our future in many ways.

As a species we are connected to all other species through the constant flow of energy and life. Although our outer forms may appear different, we are all made of the same stuff and share a common evolutionary heritage. Humans, animals, plants, and microbes are, in a very literal sense, brothers, sisters, cousins, aunts, and uncles. We share many of our genes and the same biochemical processes that keep us alive; we humans are made up of exactly the same stuff embodied in other species countless times over millions of years. The raw materials of life have been here as long as the planet has existed and living things just use them over and over again. People do not exist outside the domain of nature but are part of it and inseparable from it. Our well-being is linked to the health of our environment.

In my opinion the fundamental issue in protecting coral reef health and vitality is a lack of public understanding about coral reefs: their value to humans, how a coral reef functions, why they are vulnerable to human impact, and how they can be managed sustainably. I am convinced that if, in our heads, we appreciated the important value of reefs, their inhabitants, and the work they do in keeping the coral reefs' life support systems functioning, we would, in our hearts, feel very differently about them. Since our behavior is more affected by our hearts than our heads, such understanding would be a major advancement in seeing coral reefs protected.

Coral Reefs: Cities Under the Sea offers a unique and compelling perspective of coral reefs. Seldom can a scientist present such a creative and engaging story as has Dr. Richard Murphy. He is a curious biologist in every sense of the word. I know his story well (we began working together in 1968) as it has been tested on me, my crew, and the public who participated in our various field study programs. I am convinced his book will be a major contribution in helping students, divers, and the public better appreciate coral reefs.

When you decided to read this book, you made a good choice. Dick, with his insatiable desire to discover, to experience, to understand, will transport you on an adventure of discovery where very few have ever been. For you, he will make the profound appear obvious! Fun could be the word at times, interesting it will be all of the time, and surprising it is often. A sense of wonder will become part of the experience. Dick makes us realize that "everything is connected" in the ocean world, as in the rest of the world.

Here is a scientist, like very few, who you can understand, who dazzles his audience with the fascinating world of the coral reef. His message is conveyed eloquently in both words and images. We will learn that in the coral city there is no waste, that everything is a resource. He will help us understand how nature works—that it can work for you or against you and that it does all of this complex and laborious work for free! Dick invites you to enter the world he loves. He will make us care for it, as we should, for the well-being of our species.

PREFACE

HAVING WORKED with Jacques Cousteau from 1968 until 1994, and with Jean-Michel Cousteau continuously since 1968, I have had the good fortune of diving quite a number of reefs around the world. During these years with the Cousteaus I have been involved in doing scientific research, making films, writing articles, and teaching. Part of my job has been to communicate the observations from our expeditions and to interpret science and what we have learned on those expeditions for a wide variety of audiences through various media. Unlike many biologists who focus on the ways in which creatures and ecosystems differ, I have been fascinated by similarities. With a background in systems ecology I look for common functions performed by different critters—how they capture solar energy, how they use resources efficiently, how they form partnerships for mutual benefit, and so on.

It was on the Cousteau ship, "Calypso," in Papua New Guinea where this question of common functions became most clear to me. One afternoon I came up from a dive to find Captain Cousteau waiting on deck, as was his custom, wanting to learn what we had seen. We chatted about the diversity of fish and pigmentation of corals. Since I had just come from the Caribbean, he asked me about differences between reefs in the two regions. Of course there were many differences, including much higher biodiversity in Papua New Guinea than in the Caribbean, but I was much more impressed by the similarities between the two regions. In both there were parrotfish who stand on their tails to solicit cleaning, fiercely territorial damselfish who protect their gardens of algae, and corals of different species that have very similar forms and perform comparable functions in their respective ecosystems.

It was our custom on Calypso to meet each morning and chat about a subject of mutual interest. Captain Cousteau and I

2: An explosion of color, soft corals decorate a reef and provide refuge for basslets.

took turns choosing the subject, which ranged from the pitfalls of democracy to the role of flowering plants in the evolution of mammals.   So after this dive, Captain Cousteau said that he wanted our discussion the following morning to focus on this idea of common features of reefs and the fundamental principles that might explain those features.   During the night I visualized the various reefs I had dived in different parts of the world, thinking of their resident invertebrates and fish and reflecting on similar ways in which they appeared to meet the challenges of survival.

The next morning I began by asking Captain Cousteau to think of a number of major cities from around the world.   In those cities the faces of the residents and the street signs would be different but the basic infrastructure of the city would be the same.   Traffic would be controlled by signals at intersections, electricity would power elevators, grocery stores would sell food, police would keep order, doctors would treat patients, toilets would be connected to pipes and carry sewage somewhere, food would be produced on farms and carried to the cities by trucks, and on and on.   These basic functions would be totally predictable and, I suggested, likewise in the coral reef there are basic functions fundamental to all reefs.   We discussed this for some time, exploring where the metaphor held and broke down.   I proposed that such things as the efficient use of energy, the reuse of byproducts or waste, the importance of public health, the value of biodiversity, and the fact that all life is connected in one way or another are fundamental to all communities—whether they be human or "natural." This was the beginning of my involvement with the idea that coral reefs and cities might have something in common.

Some years ago, with Jean-Michel Cousteau, I became involved in a resort in Fiji that we attempted to make as environmentally responsible as possible.   I designed the environmental program for both operation and interpretation.   This provided a wonderful opportunity to take the city metaphor and put it into practical application——a chance to practice what I had preached!

An important goal of our involvement in this project is for

it to become an example to help other resorts and coastal developments operate in ways that would not degrade the natural environment and still be viable businesses. Thus we strived to achieve ecological and economic sustainability to prove that each is compatible with the other. After 10 years of effort we were pleased when the resort received the Conde Nast 2005 award for the best eco resort in the world.

As there was a wide variety of people involved in this project, I explained our approach as follows: The coral reef runs on solar energy and recycles almost everything. It creates almost no waste since all byproducts are used in one way or another. There are many different organisms that have important jobs and, collectively, their work keeps the community functioning through time in a relatively sustainable manner. Shouldn't these be the goals of any human enterprise as well? Certainly these goals are more environmentally sound and ought to be more economically viable as well. Thus, in Fiji we create biosystems and functional landscapes to meet our needs. In other words, we strive to form partnerships with the natural world using the free services of nature to do work for us. For example, air conditioning is not done by machines but rather by shade trees and the passive solar design of structures. A diverse suite of plants attracts predatory birds and insects. One-hundred percent of our sewages is treated naturally and either used for irrigating our landscaping or held in a pond filled with fish, shrimp, and frogs—all of which help in naturally controlling pests. This solves two problems—turning waste into a resource and reducing the need for chemical pesticides. Our landscape not only helps with air conditioning and reducing pollution, but it also provides us with food and attractive flowers.

We see these as Nature's living machines and we prefer them over human-made machines because they are cheaper; the noise they make is pleasant; they smell better; they repair and replace themselves; and they run on solar energy—for free!

To my surprise, visiting editors of *Ocean Realm* Magazine,

Charlene de Jori and Cheryl Schorp, found the concept of using "reef wisdom" to guide our green development quite interesting. After reading and publishing hundreds of articles on coral reefs by many different authors, they had never really understood the wonderful ways in which a coral reef actually does its work. They urged me to write down my story and publish it. Having been a photographer for years, it was a welcome opportunity, and I thank Charlene and Cheryl at *Ocean Realm* for the encouragement that has resulted in this book.

Lest this metaphor of using a city to help explain the workings of a coral reef be misunderstood as being anthropomorphic, I do not impose human personalities or feelings on animals but rather focus on common solutions to the more universal problems of survival we all face. A coral reef is not a city; it's a coral reef but it helps to think of a city in trying to relate and understand what is happening on a coral reef.

This book is an expansion of these simple concepts. It is organized into chapters according to general categories: power plants and farms, waste management and recycling, construction and public housing, public health, conflict and cooperation, advertising, personal lives, and social security. Each begins with a simple introduction explaining why the category is important to both human and natural communities, and each is followed by examples illustrated with photographs.

Coral Reefs: Cities Under the Sea attempts to help people better understand and appreciate the coral reef. And with a better appreciation for how reefs survive through time we may gain some useful guidance in designing our own communities to be more sustainable. In addition, since coral reefs are being destroyed by human activities on an ever-widening scale, I hope that, through a better appreciation of the marvels of the coral reef, more of us may come to love them. As Captain Cousteau said to Jean-Michel one day on a beach in the Amazon: "We protect what we love."

ACKNOWLEDGMENTS

I WOULD LIKE to thank Jen Casselle, John Morrow, Rocky Strong, and Bill Kiene for their suggestions and critical review at the early stages of this work. I appreciate especially the critical reviews and additional ideas offered by Don Potts and Bob Ginsburg.

Don Santee and Tom Ordway have been great dive buddies and associates on many expeditions around the world. Charles Vinick deserves special appreciation for the support he has provided over the years. Many of these photos were taken at the Jean-Michel Cousteau Fiji Islands Resort, and I thank Jean-Michel, Mike Freed, Larry Callahan, and the entire staff for their support. Likewise, I wish to acknowledge the opportunities provided by the Wayne Hasson and the Aggressor Fleet of Live-aboard dive boats.

To my great pleasure some of the most interesting conversations and interactions involved in this book came from Ed Breisacher, editor and publisher; I thank him for making this endeavor reality. Likewise, John Westlake has, through his design, greatly enhanced the visual appeal of my images and I appreciate his hard work.

I shall be forever thankful for the support and guidance Pam Stacey has given me over many years. Her creativity and guidance has been a constant source of inspiration.

Jean-Michel Cousteau deserves a special expression of appreciation because of the many opportunities he provided both on and off our various expeditions and projects. His encouragement and support has been vital in the creation of both images and ideas reflected in this work. It would not have been possible without him.

My children, Greg and Jeanne, have been important sources of inspiration, great dive buddies, and wonderful companions. My interactions with them in tide pools, kelp beds, and coral reefs became the inspiration to develop this work. I appreciate their patience and companionship. This book is dedicated to the next generation ... particularly my own.

INTRODUCTION

CORAL REEFS HAVE typically been characterized as highly productive, biologically diverse, and extremely complex ecosystems. They occupy only 0.1 percent of the earth's surface yet they are of high economic value to humans who live near them, providing food, resources, and income. For outsiders they are prime tourist destinations, attracting people from around the world. And for the planet they are one of its important life-support systems, contributing, as do all natural ecosystems, to keeping the planet habitable.

Scientific investigation of coral reefs has increased dramatically in recent years. For example, in 1969 at the 1st International Coral Reef Symposium, 72 scientists representing 10 different nationalities attended and presented a handful of papers. By 1977, attending scientists had risen to over 600 with more than 150 papers presented. And in 2000 at the 9th International Coral Reef Symposium held in Bali, Indonesia, there were almost 1,500 attendees from 60 countries with 1,500 papers presented. In the past, texts on marine biology characterized reefs according to their latitudinal limits and environmental conditions in which they survived, such as temperature, salinity, suspended particulate matter, light, and the like. Reef zones were established, from the deep-reef drop off and face, up to the algal ridge where waves crash. Different types of reefs were defined, including fringing reefs close to coasts, barrier reefs a bit further offshore and often with a lagoon, and coral atolls encircling a sunken volcanic island. And, of course, general groups of organisms were presented, particularly those involved in reef construction and food webs.

Although a catalogue of locations, environmental conditions, forms and components provided an appreciation of certain aspects of coral reefs, they hardly conveyed the magic and mystery of the

16

living community. Doors to such wonders have opened over the last 30 years thanks to SCUBA and sophisticated scientific techniques. Scientists are coming to appreciate not only the biodiversity of reefs but how the reef residents interact and depend on one another. Yet the public, in general, is still at the cataloguing stage of knowledge about coral reefs. Popular books are mostly limited to providing the names and geographic distributions of coral reef creatures with a general discussion about the major groups of animals. But knowing the name of a fish or invertebrate does not necessarily involve an understanding of much, certainly not the wonder of that organism's personal life or how it fits into the fantastically complex ecological web of life on a reef. I believe the most fascinating aspects of coral reefs relate to how corals and reef residents meet the challenges of survival and live together.

The focus of this book is on how a coral reef functions: the jobs of individual residents and how they collectively create a sustainable community. We will explore how corals construct the structure of this city under the sea. The wisdom involved in integrating form and function should inspire the best of architects. How corals and reef communities acquire and efficiently use energy should impress any engineer. How raw materials are acquired and utilized without causing environmental disruption or pollution ought to give hope to any environmentalist. Sociologists and psychologists might find interesting parallels between how members of reef and human communities deal with issues such as public housing, dealing with conflict, finding a mate, living together, public health, and social security And for those concerned about the future, we see reef communities existing in a dynamic equilibrium where forces of competition, destruction, and decay are balanced by cooperation, repair, and rejuvenation. Through ecological webs all creatures are inextricably bound together, each to the other, in a common destiny. Evolution and extinction go hand in hand, for as long as life existed on planet Earth spinning through eons of time.

But this is also a story about humanity and the places where we live. Coral reefs are, in many ways, like cities even though there are certainly many differences at many different levels of organization. Yet by viewing coral reefs in the context of a city we can more easily see how they operate in ways that neither undermine their own survival nor that of others elsewhere; in other words, how the variety of species collectively enhances the survival of the entire community.

There may be lessons we can take away from this perspective. We humans need help and guidance in living more sustainably. Living sustainably is important for our own survival and absolutely critical for the health of coral reefs. Humans are destroying the health and vitality of reefs worldwide, directly and indirectly. Direct threats are mostly local. Indirect threats are mostly related to global climate change, such as global warming, that is a result of how we use and waste energy. This is an issue involving us all, no matter where we live. Some consider coral reefs as the canaries of our planet just as the health of canaries in mines indicated the quality of air miners were breathing. Sick reefs may indicate a sick planet, and we cannot afford to undermine the habitability of the only place we have to live.

In the following pages we shall explore life in the coral city in greater depth. Ours will be an adventure of discovery. The subject matter is serious, but we will not take it so seriously that it won't be fun. When you finish I hope you will have a much better idea about how a coral reef functions and, based on this knowledge, how we might live a bit more gently on our planet.

3: Delicate arms of a basket star reach out for plankton.

4

CHAPTER ONE
Power Plants and Farms

SOLAR ENERGY POWERS the coral city, where buildings are alive, growing, adapting to change, repairing themselves, evolving. Here, under the sea, are simple, brainless animals called corals, creatures lacking "modern" technology but ingeniously using raw materials and sunlight to create a framework for the most magnificent structures on the planet: coral reefs. (Plate 4) This important work is accomplished with energy transfer, which is the basis of all activity in our universe.

Think of just about anything that grows (such as flowers in a garden or wheat in a field), or moves (such as cars, trains, or planes), or interacts (such as our communications systems). Take away energy and everything stops. Our human communities run primarily on solar energy that has been accumulated over millions of years, stored in organic matter that has become what we call petroleum. This petroleum "subsidy" supports our entire civilization. Without it, life as we know it would be profoundly different. At this moment in the world's history we are totally incapable of powering our present civilization on direct solar energy. A solar-powered city is the dream of futurists, environmentalists, and experts specializing in renewable energy.

Solar Collectors

The coral city runs exclusively on solar energy. This is possible because almost all the surfaces of the coral reef are covered with solar collectors—various species of plants called algae. Some take the form of underwater farms and gardens; some are thin encrustations growing over the reef foundation; and others are the

5

4: Buildings of this city under the sea are alive, growing, making food, and providing habitat for other residents. (*Porites lichen*, Fiji)

5: Elkhorn corals create the framework of the coral city, reaching outward to capture more sunlight for their algal partners. (*Acropora palmata*, Caribbean)

21

algae living inside corals. In fact, the form of many coral colonies is specially designed to promote efficient energy collection by algae.

Ultimately solar energy is converted into chemical energy stored in food and organic matter. This is the power source for all the plant and animal life of the reef. Without these solar collectors the coral reef could not exist. (Plate 5) In converting solar energy

6

into food, coral reefs are about as productive as rain forests and our "highly productive" mechanized agriculture (*1*). In addition to solar efficiency, fields of alfalfa, corn, or wheat depend on the importation of external sources of fertilizers, pesticides, and technology— on enormous amounts of energy subsidies invested in tilling the soil, in sowing seeds, and in harvesting crops. Coral reefs, on the other hand, do not depend on such external inputs to keep the community functioning smoothly. The high rates of productivity and efficiency of coral reefs are, in part, due to the architectural wisdom of corals themselves. Since sunlight comes down from above, solar collectors must be positioned on the top of the colony to receive it. To provide the greatest surface area for the absorption of sunlight,

6: In order to maximize their surface area for solar collection, some corals flare outward in the form of tabletops. (*Acropora* sp., Fiji)
7: Instead of reaching skyward for sunlight, massive brain corals provide increased surface area for its resident algae through meandering convolutions of its surface. (*Diplora labyrinthiformis*, Caribbean)
8: The green color of this brain coral is due to the presence of zooxanthellae, the algae that convert sunlight into food for the coral. (*Diplora strigosa*, Caribbean)

many corals flare into shapes resembling tabletops, arms reaching toward the sun, or leaves on a tree. (Plate 6)

Other corals, called brain corals, employ a different architectural strategy. We humans, "higher" mammals with brainpower, benefit from all the convolutions of our cerebrums. More convolutions mean more surface area for more cells to conduct more thinking. Likewise, corals need more surface area for more cells to collect more sunlight. Thus, we see an evolutionary convergence between very distantly related animals using similar strategies to meet similar needs. (Plates 7, 8)

Corals as Farmers: the Coral-Algae Relationship

The structures that enable coral animals to use solar energy are only one part of the story. Because corals are animals, and animals cannot use direct sunlight, they can only meet their energy needs by consuming other creatures. Yet, these coral animals appear to be acting like plants because, of course, they are full of plants or algae. In fact, the tissue of an individual coral animal, or polyp, may be as much as thirty-percent plant material (2). Algae residing inside the coral use sunlight and make food that they in turn share with the coral animals. These algae, called zooxanthellae, are a type of dinoflagellate, the class of Protista that forms an important part of ocean plankton, some of which act like animals, obtaining their energy from food they ingest while others use photosynthesis for their needs. Those that live inside corals are photosynthesizers. Thus, in this one group of organisms some members are categorized as animals while others are more like plants. It's the dinoflagellates that cause breaking waves to glow greenish-blue with bioluminescence, while others reproduce in great numbers, creating toxic "blooms" that cause fish kills and shellfish to be poisonous to eat.

This coral-algae relationship benefits each partner. The coral grows in forms that help algae receive more sunlight and provides shelter and essential raw materials for its internal garden of algae.

7

8

9

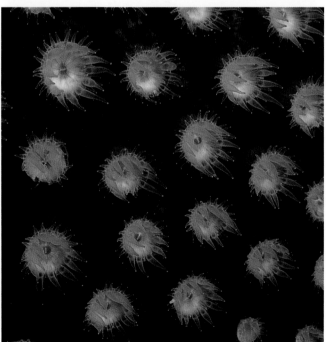

10

As animals, corals produce metabolic wastes, the byproducts of their using food, some of which comes from the algae in the first place. These wastes are the very nutrients algae need for growth. Thus, byproduct substances such as carbon dioxide, nitrogen, and phosphorus are efficiently recycled (*3*). The coral has its own wastes removed and the algae use it as fertilizer, helping the algae to convert more sunlight into more food. In some cases, as much as eighty percent of the food produced by algae may be released to the coral host (*4*). Although much of this is nitrogen-poor organic food, called "junk food" by some scientists, it is a valuable source of energy. Oxygen produced during photosynthesis becomes another form of payment by the algae to the coral for the fertilizer, and the coral in turn provides the algae with a place to live. We know this relationship is important because research has shown that zooxanthellae are necessary for a coral to construct their skeletons. When deprived of their algal partners the deposition of calcium carbonate ceases and the corals eventually die.

Corals as Predators

The nutritional benefit of having algae live inside corals is only part of the story. Being animals, corals can prey on other, external food sources as well. At night, swarms of small reef dwellers emerge to swim and crawl about the reef. Collectively these are called demersal zooplankton, which means drifting (planktos) animals (zoo) that live in association with the bottom (demersal). These are the little creatures that congregate around a diver's light at night, in much the same way as insects are drawn to a light on land. As animal tissue rich in nitrogen and phosphorus, they serve as important nutritional supplements for the corals. Since the recycling involved in the coral-algae partnership is not perfect, feeding on demersal zooplankton makes up for any loss of nutrients. This may be why so few corals have their tentacles extended during the day: In daytime, coral tissue, which is full of algae, can thus be exposed directly to sunlight without coral tentacles getting in the way. At night, when there is no solar energy available, tentacles stretch out to capture plankton.

Corals are really the supreme opportunists since they also feed on non-living sources of food. Corals have been observed feeding on drifting particles of organic material, and they even absorb dissolved organic molecules. Thus, the marvelously ingenious yet "simple," brainless corals employ incredibly efficient strategies of form and behavior to make the best use of whatever source of food is available—day and night. (Plates 9, 10).

Other Reef Farmers

Corals are not the only farmers on the reef. Giant clams are the largest clams on the planet, thanks largely to the same partnership corals have with zooxanthellae. Members of this genus of giant clams, known as *Tridacna*, are one of the two largest clam groups that have ever existed on planet Earth. (The other group is called rudist bivalves, which became extinct around 70 million years ago.) Called man-eaters by some, giant *Tridacna* clams live peacefully and, like the corals, feed on algae and also filter plankton from the water, as do most bivalves. Compared to other clams, the soft mantle of this giant clam, which constructs or secretes the shell, is greatly expanded. The zooxanthellae reside in this mantle tissue. Thus, with more mantle there is more surface area for more algae to absorb more sunlight and make more food (5). These clams even have small lens-like structures (ocelli) in their mantle through which light penetrates, giving even more light to more algae.

So, we see a remarkable convergence in strategies employed by corals and giant clams. Both grow in forms to provide a greatly expanded surface for their algal gardens to capture sunlight, and both employ recycling of animal waste to help fertilize the algae. As with the coral-algae relationship, the recycling of nutrients is essential to maintaining productivity by the algae in the clams. (Plate 11)

9: During the day many corals withdraw their tentacles, relying on their algal partners to produce food from sunlight. (*Montastrea* sp., Caribbean)

10: At night when small planktonic creatures emerge from reef crevices, corals extend their tentacles to harvest a resource rich in important nutrients lacking in the food produced by the algae. (*Montastrea* sp., Caribbean)

11: Between the drab shells of a giant clam lies the colorful mantle tissue, which secretes the shell and contains algae. (*Tridacna derasa*, Palau)

12: Like all bivalves, giant clams are filter feeders. Water enters through the opening, seen here, and passes across the gills where oxygen is extracted and plankton is filtered. (*Tridacna squamosa*, Palau)

13

14

13: The mantle of giant clams is greatly expanded, completely hiding the shells below. Zooxanthellae reside in the mantle, so more mantle means more algae to make more food. (*Tridacna squamosa*, Palau)

14: Solar collection is enhanced by the presence of tiny lens-like structures, which enable light to penetrate further into the mantle of giant clams, thus increasing opportunities for algae to make food. (*Tridacna* sp., Palau)

15: The brilliant colors of giant clam mantles are due to accessory pigments that may serve as antennae to capture sunlight of wavelengths beyond the range of chlorophyll, and as sunblocks for protection against too much light. (*Tridacna* sp., Palau)

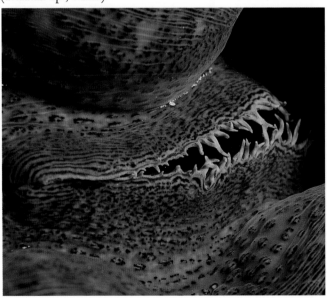

15

The Japanese, English, and French take great pride in the artistic design of their gardens. Although garden designs are beautiful and objects of contemplation, they are of little practical use. On the other hand, giant clams blend magnificent abstract beauty with an important functional purpose. If the vivid pigments in clams serve a similar function to their role in corals, they may serve both as antennae and sunblocks. As antennae they help collect solar energy at wavelengths beyond that which is absorbed by chlorophyll. And as sunblocks they can protect the clams and algae from the damaging effects of intense sunlight (6). (Plates 12, 13, 14, 15)

Regarding the man-eating stories about these clams, there is no reason swimmers and divers need fear these giants and it's doubtful

16

they can kill you. You would need to shove your foot between the shells, then wait a bit for the clam to laboriously pull in its mantle and finally close the shell. There are other, much easier ways to drown than being held under water by the weight of the clam. Although these clams can't eat humans, we *do* eat them. In fact, the harvest of giant and very old clams is a major threat to their survival as a group. Sadly, renegade poacher fishermen often invade a reef, harvesting the clams for the muscle that pulls the shells shut and departing before local people or wardens can apprehend them. On the other hand, *Tridacna* clams can be farmed and are becoming a source of sustainable income for village communities.

There are even some jellyfish that farm algae. The upside-down jellyfish, *Cassiopeia* sp., also have zooxanthellae. In order to make sure they get the most sunlight possible, the jellyfish rest on the bottom, inverted to expose their algae-bearing tentacles to the sun. Another type (*Mastigias* sp.) lives in Jellyfish Lake, Palau, and

17

actually descends at night into nutrient-rich waters to fertilize its internal gardens; then, at dawn it rises to give its algal partners the solar energy necessary to make food for both algae and jellyfish (7). (Plates 16, 17)

The same solar energy that fuels the "vegetable gardens" of corals, giant clams, and jellyfish also supports another group, the farmer damselfish. These damselfish establish territories, chasing off grazing urchins and other fish, and allowing algae to grow naturally (8). Their gardens are composed of particular species of algae since the damselfish "weed" them, keeping out undesirable species. Once established, the gardens are then fiercely protected from just about anything that approaches too close, including divers hundreds of times larger than the damselfish. Were these territorial damselfish the size of large groupers or sharks, the coral reef would indeed be a very dangerous place for divers. But they are not, and divers need only fear a nip or bump from time to time. In the photo, notice the damselfish attacking its reflection in a mirror, attempting to drive off what it thinks is another of its own species. (Plate 18)

Actually much of the reef's surface has the appearance of being relatively denuded of algae, but in reality it is covered with algae—in some cases, with a thin veneer of pink algae, like a layer of cement covering the bottom. These coralline algae cover most surfaces on the reef where corals are not living. Coralline algae are very important because they are the mortar that binds reef fragments together and solidifies the reef into one durable structure. In fact, some scientists have suggested that coral reefs be called algal reefs, since in some regions algae may be as important in reef formation as are the corals themselves (9).

On top of this layer of coralline algae there may be a turf or lawn of algae that is almost invisible because it is regularly trimmed down by the lawnmowers of the reef. All during the day, herbivorous fish cruise over the reef, nipping at the bottom. The beak of

18

16: In Jellyfish Lake, Palau, these jellyfish follow the sun during the day so algae living in their tissues can make food. Then at night the jellyfish descend to nutrient-rich waters to fertilize their internal algal gardens. (*Mastigias* sp., Palau)
17: The upside-down jellyfish orients itself so that algae, residing in the tentacles, will be exposed directly to the sun. (*Cassiopea xamachana*, Caribbean)
18: A farmer damselfish attacks what it thinks is an invader to its territory. These fish fiercely defend their gardens of algae, seen here as fuzz on the branching coral in the foreground. (*Stegastes nigricans*, Fiji)

the parrotfish and the fine teeth of the surgeonfish enable them to mow the algae down to almost nothing. Some parrotfish are particularly zealous, breaking off chunks of the reef itself, grinding up the calcium carbonate in their throats and extracting algae from the pieces of limestone (*10*). (Plates 19, 20) On most healthy reefs this destruction by parrotfish is balanced by reef growth and thus their impact is not considered detrimental to the overall ecosystem.

At night the sea urchins take over. With five calcareous jaws, the urchins forage over the reef, further trimming the algal lawn. In some areas a denuded patch on the reef indicates the home range of an urchin. Like parrotfish, urchins erode the bottom as they graze and are an important force in the erosion of reefs (*11*).

Such intensive grazing might be considered overexploitation of the resource. In fact, it is the most efficient way to go. Young organisms grow faster than old ones; therefore, keeping the young algae trimmed down prevents them from growing large and from

19: Parrotfish are herbivores and play an important role in controlling the growth of algae that could overgrow the reef and prevent the settlement of coral larvae. (*Scarus vetula*, Caribbean)

shading themselves. Consequently, by being constantly grazed, the lawn of algae is kept at its most productive growth rate (*12*).

In the coral city the buildings are alive and growing, and the rooftops are covered by gardens where waste is converted into food. Actually, most available surfaces of the reef are covered with solar collectors whether they be corals, giant clam mantles, damselfish farms, or the reef substrate carpeted with coralline and other algae. The lesson is obvious for those of us trying to live more sustainable lives. The more we utilize direct solar energy and reuse our waste as raw materials the more likely our communities will be able to maintain themselves through time without causing environmental disruption that ultimately undermines their "sustainability." For example, by integrating plants into the infrastructure of our communities, we could cover our rooftops and other unused surfaces with living solar collectors, thus efficiently using a resource otherwise totally wasted.

20: The teeth of parrotfish are fused into a beak that is strong enough to break off pieces of coral skeleton. In their throats, parrotfish have molar-like "teeth" that grind up coral to extract algae. (*Scarus vetula*, Caribbean)

CHAPTER TWO
Waste Management and Recycling

IN THE CORAL CITY there is no waste. The byproduct of every organism is a resource for another. This is seen in the relationship between corals and the algae that live inside the coral polyps. The internal recycling of nutrients between corals and algae insures that fertilizer is not lost to the outside and that algal productivity remains high. This recycling takes place completely within the coral polyp.

In the context of the larger ecosystem, we also see that there is no significant waste. The coral city sanitation department is composed of workers such as sea cucumbers and worms, who forage over the reef cleaning up, ingesting, and reusing anything left over. Efficient use and recycling by the sanitation engineers are important to the sustainability in the coral reef ecosystems. These recyclers use up all the energy in the reef's byproducts and return to the environment the raw materials that are in short supply. These raw materials are then used by plants to make more food and initiate a new cycle. (Plates 21, 22)

This efficiency is important because many reefs thrive in the midst of vast aquatic deserts of the open sea. In this "biological desert," it is the nutrients that are in short supply—so short that primary productivity, which is the conversion of solar energy into chemical energy by algae that becomes useful food for other organisms, is comparable to that of the Sahara Desert (*13*). Nutrients or fertilizer are essential for algae to thrive and serve as food for the rest of the ecosystem. Where there are no nutrients there is no

22

21: Decorating this reef is a variety of sponges that filter the water, retaining important materials within the reef ecosystem. (Caribbean)
22: Appearing like smokestacks of the reef, the role of these sponges is just the opposite of their human counterparts. Instead of releasing waste, sponges filter the water, releasing it "cleaned" of organic waste from other reef creatures. (*Aplysina fistularis*, Caribbean)

23: Parrotfish bite off chunks of reef and grind it up to extract algae inside. Parrotfish poop is mostly sand. (*Scarus* sp., Caribbean)

24: We can thank parrotfish for helping to create sand for those "pristine" beaches of paradise as their feces are largely ground-up coral. (Caribbean)

food produced; thus, nutrients limit the amount of work algae can do. In spite of nutrient limitations, coral reefs exist as highly productive oases in these deserts thanks to the sanitation engineers and their role as recyclers. In fact, recycling helps coral reefs sustain rates of productivity as high as rain forests.

Parrotfish: The Lawnmowers of the Reef

Consider again the parrotfish that serve as lawnmowers by keeping algae from dominating the surface of the reef. Have any of you who are divers ever noticed that as a scared parrotfish darts off it may leave a cloud of smoke behind? Well, you just scared the poop out of it, but in the case of parrotfish the defecated material is special. (Plate 23) In the process of their grazing on algae or corals, the parrotfish may break off pieces of the calcium carbonate. Ground up in the throat by molar-like pharyngeal teeth, this calcium carbonate is pulverized so that the organic matter can be digested. The inedible material then passes through the gut and is released as sand. In fact, a single two-foot parrotfish can produce a few hundred pounds of sand in one year. So, as you stroll along a pristine beach with "clean" white sand beneath your feet, remember where some of it came from and who to thank for it (*14*). (Plate 24)

Landfill Put to Use

Storms often convert living coral colonies into rubble and you might think that this could undermine the structural integrity of the coral city. In fact, the remnants of the coral buildings destroyed by natural events become the bricks of reef construction, filling spaces in the reef and often becoming cemented together to form a solid reef. In fact, coral and shell fragments and the remains of calcareous algae, such as the green-segmented *Halimeda* sp., can become solidified into reefs much stronger than those composed of coral skeletons alone. Geological profiles of some ancient reefs show that such cemented debris makes up a large part of the reef's foundation, as seen in large calcareous structures such as Eniwetok Atoll. (Figure 1, p. 44)

Were we humans to embrace such a strategy we would reduce landfill problems substantially by reusing our building wastes for new construction. To a limited degree, we are beginning to do this with building materials such as used bricks, tiles made from used light bulbs, cinder blocks using waste material as aggregates, wood substitute materials made with reused plastic bags and sawdust, straw bale construction, and houses made of used tires. (Even the Romans used hollow columns filled with detritus instead of solid marble.)

Sanitation Engineers

Have you divers ever marveled at what appears to be a beautiful chain of beige pearls draped over a coral head or wondered about those nice sausage-shaped structures on a sandy bottom and thought about what they might be? Well yes, they are, as you might have guessed, the fecal castings from one of the reef's sanitation engineers. (Plates 25, 26) Many sea cucumbers crawl along the bot-

25: Some sea cucumbers use oral tentacles, black, to scour the bottom for waste organic matter (detritus). (*Bohadschia graeffei*, Fiji)

26: This sea cucumber ingests sediment and extracts what is edible; "chains of pearls" draped over the reef are what comes out . . . cleaner than what went in! In this way the sea cucumber functions as a sanitary engineer, keeping the reef clean and taking advantage of what otherwise might be considered "waste." (*Bohadschia graeffei*, Fiji)

25

26

tom, ingesting huge quantities of sand. From this sediment they extract detritus, which is waste organic matter such as feces, parts of dead organisms, and mucus. In this process they perform an important ecological function. By making use of what could be considered waste products, they increase the ecological efficiency of the entire ecosystem by more fully utilizing its food resources. They also "clean up" the reef by releasing, back to the reef, sediment cleaner than it was before it passed through their digestive tracts.

According to scientists who have calculated the amount of sand passed through the bodies of sea cucumbers, the impact of sea cucumbers on the reef is not trivial. In the South Pacific relatively dense populations of sea cucumbers of more than 33 per square yard (40 per square meter), can take in and release about 34 pounds of sediment per square yard (13 kilograms per square meter) per year (*15*). This means that, for a coral reef .6 miles long (one kilometer) and 330 feet wide (100 meters), these sea cucumbers are processing more than 1,000 tons (1,100 metric tons) of sand each year, equal to more than 75 full 12-ton dump trucks!

How the reef treats such waste is in dramatic contrast to

27: These yellow sponges (*Siphonodictyon coralliphagum*) have excavated homes for themselves in a coral head (*Siderastrea siderea*) and provide a bit of shelter for this cleaner goby (*Gobisomia* sp.). One of the functions of sponges on the reef is to clean the water, removing particles as small as bacteria. (Caribbean)

28: Sea squirts (also called tunicates), like clams, use their gills both for breathing and for feeding. Water enters the incurrent opening, passes across the gills where planktonic food is extracted, and leaves through the excurrent opening. (*Clavella puertosecensis*, Caribbean)

27

28

human cities where we, believing that such waste is bad, concentrate it and then do the best we can to throw it away, hoping or assuming it will simply disappear—which it doesn't or can't. A more sustainable option for dealing with our biological waste would be to reuse it on-site in gardens, green belts, and nearby farmlands. Gigantic cities would ideally be replaced by smaller communities where people live closer to the farms and open spaces. In this way the input of goods to and through the communities would be augmented by the return of used, raw materials to the landscape. Instead of being totally detached from nature, trapped in jungles of cement and steel, people would be more connected to the living systems that have provided for their well-being (*16*).

Purifiers

Just as the sanitation engineers clean the sediments, so do the water purifiers clean the water. (Plates 27, 28, 29, 30) Sponges, clams, and sea squirts filter sea water through their bodies, extracting food (including plankton, organic particles and even dissolved organic matter), and returning to the reef ecosystem water that is cleaner

29: Purple sponges (*Nara nematifera*) surround green colonial tunicates (*Didenmum molle*). The tunicates derive their color from algae that live inside and may provide some food to their host. Living in reef crevices these filter feeding sponges and tunicates help aerate the reef by pulling in fresh water from outside. (Palau)

30: This cock's comb oyster, covered with pink sponges, is a bivalve and like its relatives is a filter feeder. (*Lopha cristagalli,* Fiji)

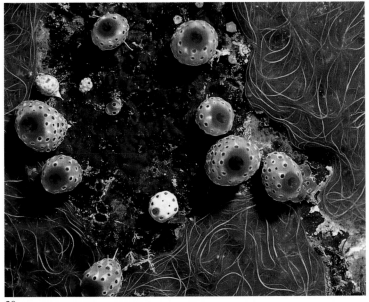
29

30

than when it arrived. By filtering the water for their own benefit they also contribute to the reef's health and vitality. Organic matter and drifting organisms that would otherwise be carried away by currents are kept within the reef ecosystem by these filter-feeders. Many water purifiers live in the rubble and in hidden spaces deep within the reef. Through their feeding currents, they ventilate the reef by bringing in oxygen and keeping the reef's recesses from becoming stagnant. This helps bacteria digest the last bits of organic matter and facilitates the return of their nutrient byproducts to the surface for algae to use as fertilizer for producing more food.

The amount of work done by these purifiers is incredible. Some sponges, for example, can remove as much as 99 percent of the bacteria from the water they filter, and some can filter their own volume of water in less than 30 seconds (*17, 18*). Imagine a hypothetical reef .6 miles long (1,000 meters) and 330 feet wide (100 meters) wide at a depth of 33 feet (10 meters). Now imagine a population of sponges, within this area, consisting of one-half liter of tissue per square meter, which is not unreasonable considering that some sponges are over one meter in diameter and more than a meter tall. This imaginary population of sponges could filter 38 million gallons of water every day, and the entire volume of water above the reef four times each day! Not bad for a solar-powered, air- and water-conditioning system that repairs and replaces itself —for free!

Recycling

One of the main attractions to diving on coral reefs is the clarity of the water. The water is so clear because there is so little phytoplankton, which is in turn the specific result of low concentrations of nutrients in the waters. The oceanic waters that bathe many coral reefs are called biological deserts because of the lack of abundant nutrients. (Plate 31) So, how can the lush and productive reefs survive in a biological desert? As mentioned earlier in this chapter, the answer involves recycling at a number of ecological levels.

At the level of the coral polyp, it is the relationship with its resident algae, where algae produce food for the coral and use the animal waste as the fertilizer. If the wastes were released to the surrounding water, the nutrients could be carried from the reef by ocean currents and lost to the ecosystem. At the larger ecosystem level the recyclers and water conditioners also help keep valuable resources from being lost to the system. Their function as recyclers

31: Although this barrel sponge (*Xestospongia muta*), nestled among these sea plume gorgonians (*Pseudopterogorgia* sp.) may not move, it is doing an incredible amount of work filtering water. Some species can pull a volume of water through their bodies every 30 seconds. Collectively a reef's population of sponges may filter millions of gallons of water every day. (Caribbean)

minimizes loss and maximizes productivity. Of course, there is leakage and these losses are made up by such things as blue-green algae, which can convert nitrogen gas into biologically useful forms, and currents that bring fresh raw materials such as phosphorus to reef communities.

The recyclers are not altruistic, though. At the individual level they are doing work to stay alive and reproduce. Yet at a larger community level they are performing important functions that benefit the entire ecosystem. As with most of the reef's residents, they are doing multiple jobs at once: one selfish and another with benefits beyond self.

Our modern human cities don't fare well in terms of efficiency and recycling, and for now efficient recycling is not high on our priority list, at least in most countries—although it is a topic of major concern and a high priority in a few countries on our planet. Ours is still a throw-away mentality. But on planet Earth you cannot really throw anything away; it is just put somewhere else. We do not yet realize, as a generally shared commitment, that this approach is inappropriate. Our sanitation departments are dedicated more to protecting people from disease and getting rid of garbage and burying or dumping personal wastes and chemicals into landfills or into the sea.

As we continue to consume and deplete more and more resources, we will no longer be able to afford the luxury of wasting nutrients contained in our domestic waste. Soon we shall be faced with the question of how to reuse waste to fertilize and irrigate green belts and farmland, to improve crop productivity, and to find better ways to reduce costs by eliminating the problems of where to put waste. As on the coral reefs, in the future we are likely to be designing communities where recycling and food production are integrated into "edible landscaping." (Plate 32) In these more enlightened communities their slogan may be "Garbage is good!"

32: In the coral city waste is recycled—a resource to enhance on-site production. Yet it is not a completely closed system and there are some losses. Balancing this are residents, like these basslets that feed on plankton drifting in from the open sea, converting oceanic resources into reef resources. (*Pseudanthias squammipinnis*, Fiji)

CHAPTER THREE
Construction and
Public Housing

T HE LARGEST STRUCTURES on our planet created by living things are coral reefs—more massive and taller than the Sears Tower in Chicago or the pyramids in Egypt. At their tops coral buildings remain alive—growing, adapting, and reproducing themselves through eons of time. Not bad for simple animals that have a nervous system but lack a brain. But corals are not the only builders of living structures our oceans have known.

The first reefs existed more than a billion years ago and were constructed by blue-green algae, a type of bacteria forming strange, pillar-shaped structures called stromatolites. Today, stromatolites are found in the Bahama Islands, Australia, and Mauritius. During the last 500 million years a succession of other builders, including sponges, corals, worms, and bivalves, have constructed reefs. Corals evolved at least 500 million years ago, and a type now extinct, called rugose corals, were involved in creating the first coral reefs. The great Permian extinction, about 250 million years ago, wiped them out but in their place evolved the Scleractinian corals of which most of our reefs are made today. Most of the coral genera we see today had evolved by about 35 million years ago and contemporary reefs are even younger in geological terms. The Great Barrier Reef probably began to grow only 18 million years ago and most reefs elsewhere are only a few million to a few thousand years old (*19*). Although modern corals are not the first reef builders, they are among the most impressive. (Plate 33)

33: Using renewable solar energy and recycling raw materials, corals (*Turbinaria mesenterina*) create living apartment buildings for residents (*Lutjanus biguttatus*) of the coral city. (Palau)

The Atoll

Although atolls are much less common than other reef forms, the story of their formation reflects the fascinating dynamics of how coral reefs grow. An atoll is a ring of coral reefs surrounding a large lagoon. When Charles Darwin was exploring the South Pacific in the mid-1830s, he noticed what seemed to be a gradual transition from recent volcanic islands with reefs close to shore, to islands where a ring of coral encircled an open lagoon, and finally to a ring of reefs surrounding a lagoon with no island at all. He speculated that the volcanic islands were the foundation on which corals grew and that through geologic time the islands sank, or subsided, until the island was totally submerged, leaving only a ring of coral. His theory remained just a theory until the 1960s when an accident of history moved scientific knowledge forward and proved him correct.

Eniwetok Atoll just happens to be one of the most well-known and thoroughly studied coral islands. From 1947 to 1952 the American military held atomic and hydrogen bomb tests on this atoll in the Marshall Islands. As part of that operation, scientists sought to test Darwin's theory of atoll formation. After drilling holes to over 2,000 feet and then over 3,000 feet deep, and finding only limestone, they finally hit something much harder at 4,610 feet (20). Ultimately, it was determined that the drill hit basalt, the volcanic foundation on which corals have built the most impressive structure ever created by a living thing. In other words, these drillings showed that on top of a large volcanic mountain, corals had created a huge limestone cap more than 4,600 feet high and that the top of this mountain had once been at the sea surface and subsequently subsided to the depth at which the coral-basalt interface was discovered. But the fact that the reef of Eniwetok is more than 20 miles in diameter suggests that height is much less noteworthy than the volume of this structure. The coral cap built from the calcareous rem-

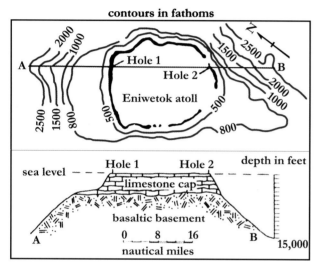

Figure 1: Eniwetok atoll, created by corals, is 70,000 times greater by volume than the largest Egyptian pyramid. (© *McGraw-Hill Encyclopedia of Science and Technology.* Reproduced with permission of The McGraw-Hill Companies)

(Photo: Courtesy, John T. Westlake)

nants of the successive reefs has become a limestone structure of tremendous proportions. Eniwetok turns out to be more than ten times higher and at least 70,000 times larger by volume than the largest of the three pyramids (composed of the remains of one-celled planktonic animals called foraminifera) at Giza, near Cairo, Egypt! A truly impressive structure created by "primitive" coral polyps." (Figure 1)

The Coral Home—the Corallite

But a gigantic volume of limestone rock is not what attracts us to the reef. Rather, it is the living creatures, the corals themselves, that deserve our attention. (Plate 34)

A coral is a colony of individual polyps—each a sister, or brother, of all other polyps of the colony. They begin life as most animals do, with the union of sperm and egg. After fertilization, embryos develop into tiny larvae, called planulae. These larvae are carried by currents to other reefs and even to other islands, enabling corals to establish communities elsewhere. The larvae are covered with hair-like cilia, which give them limited mobility and enable them to search for hard surfaces on which to settle. This is a selective process of tasting and touching the bottom to find just the right habitat.

When each larva has settled, it begins to construct beneath itself a circular home of calcium carbonate called a corallite. Within each home are many supporting walls, called septa, radiating inward toward the center. Their arrangement is unique to each species of coral and helps scientists identify and differentiate species. (Plate 35)

As the coral animal (called a polyp) grows, it extends its tissue outward to form additional sister polyps. This budding of polyps is a form of asexual reproduction. The polyps also grow upward and, like the chambered nautilus, many create separations or floors as the

34: Coral heads are created by hundreds to thousands of individual coral polyps, each making their contribution by fabricating their homes of calcium carbonate. The living coral constitutes a thin veneer of tissue over layers and layers of skeletal material previously laid down. (*Porites* sp., Hawaii)

35: Pairs of sister polyps show how corals asexually reproduce, where one polyp divides into two and so on to create a coral colony. All individuals are thus clones, i.e., exact genetic replicas, sharing the same genes. (*Eusmilia fastigiata*, Caribbean)

polyps grow. Since most of the space in a coral's home is left open for the animal to occupy, coral skeletons are relatively porous. (Figure 2)

Coral Architects

Corals are truly supreme examples of the architectural integration of form and function. Collectively, corals become the buildings and building materials of the reef. Each species can be compared to a type of building designed by a different architect, each with its own particular style. Some architects create massive structures, often resembling skyscrapers; others construct delicate leaf-like forms. Still, all of the reef-building corals capture sunlight for their algal partners and thus, in many species, the architecture depends on the amount of sunlight available. (Plate 36) Wave surge also influences the architectural design, causing coral colonies to become more and more sturdy and stunted as wave impact increases. Both coral reefs and human cities exist where they do because of environmental conditions favorable to their inhabitants. For the reefs, optimal temperature, light, salinity, and water movement are important. For humans, many cities have been built at sites affording protection from invaders, a valuable resource such as water, or a river for trade and transportation. Thus, in the ocean we see reefs built upon reefs during thousands to millions of years. Likewise, on land many cities have been constructed on the sites of former cities revealed by archaeological excavations that show layer after layer of evidence for prior occupation over hundreds to thousands of years.

Roommates and Other Residents

In constructing homes for themselves, corals provide public housing for a remarkable diversity of other reef animals. These undersea apartments are often densely occupied by a variety of fish that come and go according to schedules characteristic of each spe-

Figure 2: As a coral polyp grows, it creates horizontal partitions, only occupying the uppermost part of the skeleton. This results in a coral skeleton being relatively porous, with more empty space than solid calcium carbonate. The inset shows the tip of a coral tentacle. (Courtesy of J. E. N. Veron, *Corals of the World* [2000]. Artist: Geoff Kelly)

cies. Christmas tree worms and feather-duster worms decorate the coral buildings, spending their entire lives in their homes. Deeper inside the buildings are residents we seldom see, such as sponges and clams that excavate their own chambers. Others such as crabs, shrimps, and worms come and go under the cover of darkness. In one coral colony, 1,441 worms representing 103 species were found,

36: Damselfish hover above a table coral, quickly retreating to the shelter of the reef when danger approaches. Corals, as reef architects, create structures that provide both maximum surface for their symbiotic algae to collect sunlight and habitat for an incredible diversity of fish and invertebrate residents. (Reef, Fiji Islands)

along with hundreds of other creatures including crabs, amphipods (sea fleas), shrimps, and brittle stars (*21*). (Plate 37)

One of the corals most commonly used in scientific investigations, *Stylophora pistilata*, has a remarkable variety of room mates. Research has shown that this single species is home to gall crabs, boring clams (*Lithophaga*, i.e., *litho*, rock; *phaga*, eater), *Trapezius* crabs, barnacles, Christmas tree worms, and damselfish species, though not all of these species are freeloaders (*22*). Some could be considered parasites, such as *Lithophaga*, which weakens the coral skeleton as it excavates its home. But there is another aspect to their presence. Deep within a colony there is very little water circulation, and at night, under calm conditions, those spaces can become oxygen depleted. Yet, when "boring" clams are present, their feeding currents bring fresh, oxygenated water into the spaces deep within the colony and may actually be of benefit to the coral. Such are the complex interconnections and interdependencies of creatures living together on coral reefs.

37: Empty space in the form of reef crevices and caves is an extremely important refuge for fish, like these schoolmasters, when they are not out on the reef hunting or foraging for food. (*Lutjanus apodus*, Caribbean)

Sharing Space

Another dimension of the reef's public housing system is the efficient use of space, where the same crevices are used by different fish depending on the time of day. In the daytime cardinalfish and squirrelfish may use a crevice for shelter; after they leave to forage at night, the same space may be occupied by damselfish, surgeonfish, triggerfish, wrasses, and parrotfish for night-time sleeping quarters (*23*). This process of space sharing is extremely important because many of these species need protection from nocturnal predators such as eels and sharks. (Plate 38)

Whether it be a human or coral reef community, we are most familiar with residents that are active in the daytime. But there are many residents that have adapted to night life, like shift workers who come out under cover of darkness. In fact, the demersal zooplankton, mentioned in Chapter One as the small creatures on which corals feed at night, supports a whole community of predators who likewise emerge at night to take advantage of this food resource.

38: When the more protected reef apartments are occupied, some fish like this puffer just take a nap on whatever "bed" can be found. (*Arothron nigropunctatus*, Palau)

39: Although many reef creatures withdraw at night, the emergence of reef plankton (demersal zooplankton) offers a rich source of food for basket stars, which emerge after dusk and outstretch their branched arms to grab shrimp, worms, and other plankton that swim by. (*Astrophyton muricatum*, Caribbean)

40: Sponges, like this barrel sponge (*Xestospongia testudinaria*), are home to an incredible diversity of creatures ranging from the smallest, such as bacteria and algae, to larger species like sea cucumbers (*Synaptula* sp., Bali).

41: Because sponges pull so much water through their bodies as they feed, it is likely that larger particles are retained on the outside and thus attract these "free-loading" synaptid sea cucumbers. These sea cucumbers have tiny anchor-shaped spicules in their skin, which enable them to "hook" on to the bottom, or sponge, as they forage for food. (Same species as in Plate 40)

One of the most dramatic nocturnal residents is the basket star, a member of the class of echinoderms called brittle stars. In the daytime it looks like a mass of worms all tightly wrapped up into a blob. At night the basket star slowly emerges, perches itself on a coral pinnacle, and unfolds all of its wormy arms to entrap the nocturnal zooplankton. With thousands of delicate branches, the outstretched arms of basket stars magnificently decorate the reef in living, kinetic art. (Plate 39)

Living Together

Not surprisingly, corals aren't the only species on the reef that provide public housing. Sponges are home to an incredible number and diversity of tenants. (Plates 40, 41) One researcher carefully examined all of the animals living in a large loggerhead sponge and discovered that the sponge could be home to more than 17,000 animals, with 16,000 of them being snapping shrimps (*24*). A Caribbean sponge (*Spheciospongia vesparia*) has been shown to house more

40

41

42: Contact with this barrel sponge (*Xestospongia muta*) can be very irritating to the skin. Thus any creature, like these feather duster worms (*Branchiomma* sp.), which can tolerate or adapt to the sponge's defense, may benefit from the association. (Caribbean)

than 3,000 crustaceans and worms of 15 different species, not to mention thousands to millions more microscopic algae, protozoa, and bacteria (*25*). (Plate 42)

Even empty space is not wasted in the coral city. Some fish are totally dependent on the homes created by other animals and left empty upon their death. Many worms and some molluscs bur-

43

43: Christmas tree worms (*Spirobranchus giganteus*) can excavate a home for themselves in a living coral. The gills are exposed, but the body of the worm extends down into the coral. When the worm dies, the hole remains and becomes a perfect home for fish like this blenny (*Acanthemblemaria* sp.). (Caribbean)

44: For some fish like this blenny, holes left by worms are habitat for the fish. Without the worms there would be no holes and thus no refuge for the blennies. (*Cirripectes* sp., Fiji)

44

row into the hard coral and construct tubes in which they live. A variety of blenny species is totally dependent on these second-hand homes for their own survival; they wait in their protective dwellings, darting out only to grab bits of food that drift past. (Plates 43, 44)

Empty snail shells are also not wasted but are very important vacant mobile homes to hermit crabs. Unable to create their own hard shell, or exoskeleton, to protect their soft abdomens, hermit crabs live in second-hand homes made by snails. This means that even unoccupied shells become the future homes of hermit crabs . . . bad news for "environmentally responsible" shell collectors.

45: This anemone hermit crab (*Dardanus pedunculatus*) has decorated its shell with anemones (*Phyllodiscus* sp.) whose stinging tentacles serve as protection against predators. (Fiji)

46: The hermit crab/sea anemone relationship benefits the anemone as well as the crab. By dragging its tentacles as the crab lumbers across the bottom, the anemone is getting greater access to food than if it were attached to something immobile. (Same species as in Plate 45)

As if a shell weren't enough protection for the hermit crab, some species decorate their shells with stinging anemones for additional protection. The anemones don't just happen to reside on the shells. They are stroked by the crabs as inducement to let go of the bottom, and then the crab gently holds the anemone on its shell until the anemone attaches (*26*). When the crab moves on to a larger shell, it takes its roommates with it. This is most likely a mutualistic relationship where each partner benefits. Certainly the crab gets additional protection; being attached to a moving home provides the anemone with greater opportunities for catching food. (Plates 45, 46)

The bats in your attic or spiders under your house are pretty much free loaders. Although they prey on pests, they may not directly contribute much, nor take much, from you personally. Such commensal relationships are common on the reef as well. For example, echinoderms (sea stars and their relatives) serve as particularly good homes for other species. Feather stars serve as home to worms, crabs, shrimp, and fish. (Plate 47, 49, 50) Sea urchins may have perfectly camouflaged shrimp living among their spines. Sea cucumbers are home to scale worms and shrimp (Plate 48), and a species of pearlfish may even inhabit the cucumber's anal cavity. Quite an experience for both partners! There is also a parasitic snail that is commonly found on some sea cucumbers.

The Whip Coral

One of the most impressive examples of public housing on the reef is whip coral, also known as wire coral. These colonies of polyps, which are most closely related to black coral, create a very hard skeleton of proteinaceous material and grow as a single, slender stalk reaching out into the water from the reef. This adaptation enables them to expose their food-catching polyps to currents. It also provides a perfect site for other species that want to be exposed to more food, yet need a stable base on which to live. Some species

47

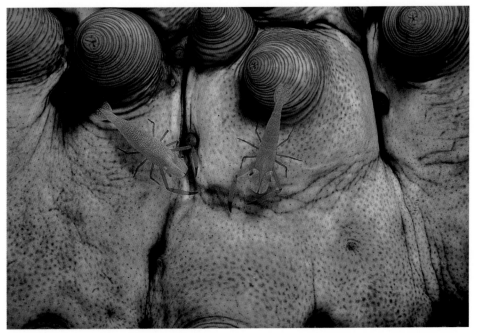

48

47: Perfectly adapted by color and behavior are two crabs, called elegant squat lobsters (*Allogalathea elegans*), that spend their lives in their resident feather star. (*Oxycomanthus* sp., Fiji)

48: This sea cucumber (*Stichopus* sp.), like most of its relatives, is not particularly tasty to many reef residents and thus a safe home to a variety of hitchhikers. These shrimp (*Periclimenes imperator*) scurry about its surface probably feeding on organisms living in the sediment rather than on the sea cucumber itself. (Fiji)

49: Feather stars have been decorating reefs for as long as corals have been building them. The earliest fossil remains of feather stars (crinoids) come from sediments over 500 million years old. (*Oxycomanthus* sp., Fiji)

50: Relatives of sea stars and sea urchins, this feather star (*Stephanometra* sp.) crawls out of reef crevices at night to extend its delicate, feather-like arms to feed on plankton. (Fiji)

51

of fish also find it a perfect place to lay eggs, for there may be fewer crawling predators on a whip coral as compared to the reef surface. (Plate 51) For example, the golden damselfish seeks out whip corals, nips off the polyps, and exposes a hard clean surface on which to lay eggs. After the female lays her eggs, the male assumes guard duty and defends them against predators. (Plate 52)

Unlike this damselfish, which only occupies space during the nesting period, the whip coral goby is a permanent resident on its whip coral. Certainly, these fish harm the whip coral, but generally the areas they clean for their nests are not extensive. Another free-loader only found on the whip coral is a species of barnacle that also takes over a small area of the skeleton. And there is a species of shrimp perfectly camouflaged like the whip coral that doesn't appear to harm its host; this shrimp and the whip coral goby are very observant and quickly move to the opposite side of the whip

52

51: Extending out from the reef is a whip coral (*Cirrhipathes* sp.) that has become a nesting site for this golden damsel-fish. (*Amblyglyphidon aureus*, Fiji)
52: Here the golden damselfish has nipped off the tissue of the whip coral, leaving a clean, black surface on which the female has laid eggs (silver dots on the coral). The male will protect the eggs for a week or so until they hatch, where-upon the young will be on their own. (Same species as in Plate 51)

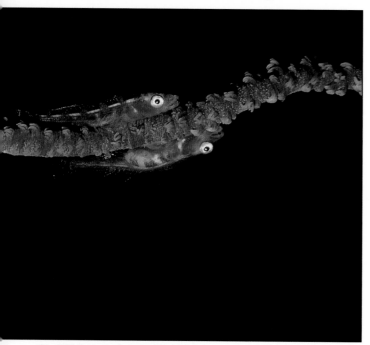

53: Whip corals are both home and nesting site for whip coral gobies (*Bryaninops yongei*) who spend their lives associated with a single whip coral. (*Cirripathes* sp., Fiji)

coral when a diver or predator approaches. Finally, there are anemones and a coral species that seem to take over the skeleton of dead whip corals. So the whip coral is one species that is a vital nesting site or home to at least six other species! (Plates 53, 54)

Remodeling the City

Communities are not static. Whether they be towns, rain forests, or coral reefs, there is a constant adjustment of species, relationships, and structures, and this adjustment is influenced by external forces and by interactions among the residents themselves. Ecologists have now studied some ecosystems long enough to understand that change is natural and important. So we should not be surprised to see that there are forces of destruction at work on the coral reef.

The most easily observed example of the forces remodeling the coral city may be seen in the intertidal notch common to uplifted limestone coastlines. Although most people assume wave ac-

54: Even after death, a whip coral is still important to the reef community, as it is often inhabited by anemones, which extend their tentacles to feed on plankton at night. (*Amphianthus* sp., Fiji)

tion has been the erosive force creating this feature, the "notch" appears to be very well developed in areas totally protected from waves, such as the innermost Rock Islands of Palau. There, one can swim or kayak among a beautiful and bizarre labyrinth of mushroom-shaped islands capped by forests. Exploration of the notch reveals a dense community of sponges, bivalves, chitons, snails, urchins, and other creatures grazing mostly on algae. Even algae can be an erosive force, releasing acids that dissolve away the limestone. Collectively, all these humble little creatures constitute a major geological force affecting the contour of coastlines (*27*). (Plate 55)

Below the tides, other "demolition crews" erode, destroy, and remodel the coral city. Most of the species involved in the reef's demolition do their work during the process of feeding or creating a home for themselves. Although such activities destroy the coral skeleton, in most cases they are not destructive to the ecosystem as a whole. These demolition crews include a variety of boring and grazing animals.

55: The notch of this limestone coastline and small island in the background is the work of bio-eroding creatures such as snails, chitons, and urchins. (Fiji)

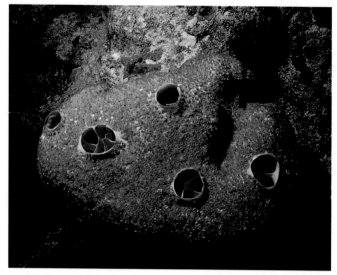

56: This red boring sponge has completely taken over a coral and probably reduced the coral's solid skeleton to a brittle and spongy mass underneath. (*Cliona delitrix*, Caribbean)

57: The architecture of these corals (*Monastrea annularis*) has been altered by these orange icing sponges (*Mycale laevis*), which, from underneath, have caused the corals to grow in "abnormal" forms. (Caribbean)

Some sponge species, for example, can have a significant impact on reef structure and even on its architecture. Feeding on plankton and not being able to move, sponges may appear to be among the reef's most passive residents. Actually they are among the reef's most chemically active group, using their chemicals to deter predators and prevent disease. In addition, sponges produce chemicals used to excavate their homes. The process involves special cells that extend into the limestone by secreting enzymes and acids to excavate a tiny chip of calcium carbonate. The cell with the chip then moves back through the sponge to its exterior and is expelled (*28*). Although some sponges do their work from the surface, most are imbedded below, inside the coral skeleton. On some reefs, 40 percent of the sediments are the result of sponge excavations (*29*). Thus, the true extent of coral demolition by sponges is seldom obvious to divers since the only evidence of the presence of sponges lies in the red or yellow dots on the surface of a dead coral branch where they pull in water for feeding and breathing.

The consequence of these excavations, which serve as a protective living chamber inside the coral skeleton, is that corals become riddled with spaces and are thus weakened. Such eroded corals are vulnerable to wave action and can break off in storm surges. Although this is not particularly good for the corals, it does facilitate one of the methods of coral reproduction: fragmentation. Broken pieces of living coral can be carried by wave action to other parts of the reef, settle in depressions, and re-establish themselves as viable colonies. This mode of reproduction or dispersal has some advantages since the new colony has a head start and is certainly less vulnerable than an individual larva that could be easily grazed by a predator or smothered by algae or sediments. (Plate 56)

Some sponges directly control the architectural construction of the reef. As they grow from underneath the coral, they cause the coral to change its growth form or morphology (*30*). What effect this has on the coral is unknown, but it explains why some corals have different forms when they are in the presence of these sponges. (Plate 57)

Herbivores scour the reef constantly, mowing the algal turf down to a thin layer of almost invisible fuzz. In the process, these herbivores erode the reef. Parrotfish often bite off pieces of dead coral, grind it up, and release it as sand. Sea urchins can also be extremely effective in eroding reefs, and some sea urchins actually create grooves and tunnels in the reef from generations of grazing. (Plate 58) Algae grow in these grooves, and in these tunnels the

58: Some sea urchins are major reef eroders as indicated by the grooves that these urchins have created for themselves. In some cases, generation after generation of urchins inhabit the same excavations, deepening them and weakening parts of the reef. (*Echinometra mathaei*, Hawaii)

59: Most boring clams, important excavators of coral skeletons, are visually just that—boring! In contrast, the coral clam also creates a home inside corals, but rivals the giant clams for beauty. Red eyes stand out like jewels against the blue and purple mantle of the clam. (*Pedum spondyloidum*, Fiji)

urchins gain a certain degree of protection from predators. Before their die-off in the early 1980s, an extremely dense population of long-spined urchins living on the fringing reefs of Barbados was eroding 23 lbs of calcium carbonate per square yard per year (9 kg/ m²/yr) (*31*). This means that for a reef .6 miles long and 330 feet wide (one kilometer long by 100 meters wide), 900 tons (1,000 metric tons) of sediment was being produced, enough to fill over 60 full 12-ton dump trucks in just one year. This destruction, however, is not typical for most reefs.

Other reef excavators might be considered the termites of the reef. One group is the bivalves, referred to above as the *Lithophaga* (rockeaters), which burrow into corals and the reef substrate. They are the boring clams (some people think all clams are "boring," but bivalve experts very much appreciate these marvelous creatures) that use both mechanical and chemical action to create a protective home for themselves. (Plate 59) The clams eventually become prisoners in their excavated home, when they grow larger than the hole they create for breathing and feeding. Many sponges also excavate the reef, creating chambers and galleries for themselves. Both the clams and sponges feed on plankton from the water pumped in from outside and filtered through their gills.

These reef "termites" perform several valuable functions: They participate in the reef's demolition by weakening coral skeletons. On the other hand, the chambers left open by these excavators become important homes to many other creatures, such as crustaceans, worms, and microbes. The labyrinth of spaces created by these excavators inside corals constitutes an important habitat for water conditioners to purify the reef's water in a protected environment. Renowned geologist Dr. Robert Ginsburg said, "The variety of life on the surface of a coral reef holds one's attention so completely that it takes considerable experience to realize that most of the bulk volume of a reef is empty space" (*32*). Quite true, but it is also true that, rather than being just empty space, these cavities are an integral and essential element of the reef ecosystem as a refuge and habitat for reef creatures, just as apartments, basements, and interior office spaces provide habitable areas in our city buildings and factories. (Plate 60)

60: Even dead coral is not wasted or useless. Here a dead table coral has become a perfect site for new colonies to become established. In this way, the process of inner city "redevelopment" continues, creating new public housing from the old. (Fiji)

On most reefs, there is a balance between the forces of destruction and growth, but there are situations where destruction exceeds growth, as just mentioned above in the example of the long-spined urchins on the fringing reefs of Barbados. Along the Pacific coast of Panama so many corals have been eliminated by warm water from El Niño events that the demolition crews have a distinct advantage over the builders. The seaward reefs of Uva Island, Panama, were producing more than 17,600 lbs (8,000 kg) of calcium carbonate per year before the 1982-83 El Niño. When the event was over, the reef was losing almost 11,000 lbs (5,000 kg) per year, due to the lack of corals and the continued presence of grazing urchins, fish, and other fauna. But there has been some interesting relief. Where damselfish have their gardens and actively keep out the herbivores, reef erosion was reduced by 4,400 lbs (2,000 kg) of calcium carbonate per year (*33*).

Since there are so many organisms participating in the reef's demolition, one wonders if their activities may be important to the long-term well being of the reef. Just as forest fires are a natural way to rejuvenate a forest, so the reef's demolition crews may work to provide new space for other species to establish themselves and eliminate those species that dominate space to the exclusion of others. Considering the long history of reefs, we can be confident that the effects of these demolition crews are not sufficiently detrimental to jeopardize the entire community; otherwise, the reefs would not survive.

In the coral city the creation of public housing involves a dynamic process of growth, the sharing of space and resources, architectural and structural readjustment, construction and destruction, and community rejuvenation. (Plate 61)

61: Life and death, growth and decay, destruction and rejuvenation—in a healthy reef these natural processes are balanced in a dynamic equilibrium that helps the coral city adapt to environmental change. (Fiji)

CHAPTER FOUR
Public Health

J UST ABOUT ALL living things are seen as a meal by some other life form. Not all predators, though, eat all their prey; some just nibble. This limited predation strategy insures the availability of future meals. Numerous human parallels come to mind and include the harvesting of fruit from trees and the milking of cows; in these cases, the living victims are left alive to produce again. Many parasites and diseases that infect animals are nibblers of sorts. Generally, these disease organisms do not kill their hosts but just extract some energy to survive and reproduce. Hosts, on the other hand, are not particularly happy about this since these nibblers create all kinds of trouble and suffering. As a consequence, we humans have created medicines and health services to rid ourselves of these unwanted free-loaders.

Reef Doctors

Coral-city residents are also vulnerable to predators, parasites, and diseases. Just as people get sick and go to a doctor for help, so do fish. (Plate 62) Fish are parasitized by isopods (pillbug-like crustaceans), copepods, worms, and other creatures. Fish are also vulnerable to infections caused by bacteria and fungi. For parasites and infections affecting the outside surface of fish, there is medical help from health professionals. These reef doctors are often called "cleaners"—shrimp and fish that "clean" their hosts of external parasites. Patients often must wait some time to be treated as there is great demand for health care, just as with our own doctors. Fish often line up, waiting their turn to be cleaned, and some reef doctors may see as many as 2,300 patients in one day. So much for

62: On a coral reef, the analogue of a doctor's office is called a "cleaning station" where public health services are offered. Here a bluestriped grunt (*Haemulon sciurus*) opens wide to be serviced by a cleaner goby. (*Gobiosoma* sp., Caribbean)

63

64

63: Attached to the head of this black-bar soldier fish (*Myripristis jacobus*) is a parasitic cymithid isopod (*Anilocara* sp.). Fish are subject to many other types of parasites and diseases, giving cleaners many opportunities to earn a good living as they provide an important "public" service. (Caribbean)

64: For full service, a Nassau Grouper (*Epinephelus striatus*) visits a cleaning station where a cleaner goby (*Gobiosoma* sp.) and this juvenile Spanish hogfish (*Bodianus rufus*) are at work. When the Spanish hogfish reaches maturity, it will cease being a cleaner and instead feed on reef crustaceans, molluscs, and brittle stars. (Caribbean)

bedside manners (*34*). These doctors are given access to the "private places" of fish and are allowed to enter the mouths and gill chambers to do their work. Some are specialists, preferring certain species of patients and certain parts of their bodies. (Plate 63) Although scientists have had a hard time proving that the activities of these cleaners actually benefit the patient, recent research has shown that cleaner wrasses do remove substantial numbers of parasites known to do their hosts harm (*35*). (Plate 64)

There is, however, one major difference between these two groups of health practitioners. Reef doctors perform their services for free! In fact, they take as payment that which is removed from their patients, such as parasites or diseased tissue. For some species of cleaners, the "rewards" are their main source of food. In this creative approach to health care, reef doctors prevent further contamination of the reef from pests and pathogens by eating medical waste! For this option AMA (American Medical Association) endorsement is highly unlikely. The fact that cleaners are common on almost all reefs worldwide indicates the importance of public health services in the coral city.

Natural Defenses

Sponges pay their way as residents by filtering water through their porous bodies. Certainly, this benefits the reef because water is purified in the process and organic matter is retained in the reef system rather than being lost to passing currents. But imagine spending your life breathing inner-city air and drinking water from the streets. To survive such a lifestyle, one had better have a pretty good immune system. Not being able to move also presents problems: What do you do if your neighbors try to encroach on your living space? Sponges, thus, must defend their living space from encroachment by neighbors. (Plate 65)

It appears that sponges have resolved these problems by hav-

65: All species must defend themselves from attack by disease, predators, and competitors. Thanks to its biochemistry, the orange sponge (*Cliona delitrix*), lower left, invades a coral (*Siderastrea siderea*) effectively competing for space and deterring predators. The purple areas on the coral indicate it is also suffering from disease. (Caribbean)

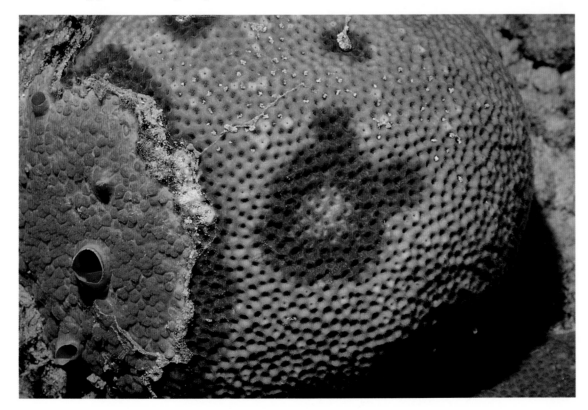

ing an extremely effective system of chemical defenses. They have anti-viral, anti-bacterial, and anti-fungal chemicals that protect them from the diseases they may receive from the water they filter (*36*). Some sponges also exude an "aura" of chemicals that deter others from growing too close and, when wounded, some sponges release defensive chemicals from 10 to 100 times the normal rate (*37*). Some sponge chemicals can even kill coral tissue and prevent zooxanthellae from producing food. The fact that some soft corals also use this strategy is indicated by the "buffer zones" or spaces separating colonies. The chemical deterrents released by some soft corals can cause tissue death, avoidance responses, and growth inhibition in other species. (Plate 66)

Sponges are presently under intense investigation by biomedical researchers as they search the reefs for sources of new drugs (*38*). Of all invertebrates studied so far, sponges, and probably the bacteria living within them, produce the largest number of what scientists call secondary metabolites (chemical byproducts resulting from one metabolic process that have become useful in a new way). The sponges presumably have modified these chemicals for defense.

Sponges are already used by non-human species for their medical benefits. To avoid being nibbled by mosquitoes, we use a repellent; likewise, some reef residents use sponges for protection. For instance, some flatworms and sea slugs do not have built-in chemical deterrents and must get them elsewhere, just as humans do; in their case they go to the reef's pharmacy—sponges. And, since they have developed tolerance to the sponge's toxic chemicals, they can graze on the sponges for food and save the noxious chemicals for their own defense (*39*). Having "stolen" these chemical repellents, they can crawl about the reef relatively immune from predation. This strategy most likely has enabled the sea slugs or nudibranchs (*nudi*, naked; *branch,* gill) to discard the heavy and energetically expensive shells of their ancestors, the snails, and cruise around "naked." (Plates 67, 68)

66: Sponges are the reef's pharmacy as they produce many chemicals to ward off bacteria, fungi, and predators. As they "prospect" reefs for new drugs, scientists are finding sponges hold great promise in helping us protect ourselves from infection and tumors. (Caribbean)

67

Sickness, Disease, and Plagues

Fishes and invertebrates do get sick, and one type of reef illness is of particular concern to people—coral diseases, which are on the rise. Sick buildings mean sick communities. On one hand, there are advantages to having a city of living buildings: They can grow, adapt, and repair and even replicate themselves. But a city of living buildings is vulnerable if the buildings get sick. Like all living things, corals are subject to stress that can lead to infections, illness, and even death. The impact of humans on reefs is becoming a critical issue as many human activities are known to stress corals. Increased sedimentation from deforestation and coastal disruption as well as increased nutrients from deforestation, agricultural runoff, sewage, and pollution in general can harm corals (*40*). There appears to be a variety of coral illnesses, and the more we learn about them, the more we see connections to human influences.

Black-band disease results from blue-green algae (Cyano-bacteria: *Phormidium corallyticum*), along with a group of other micro-organisms growing around a coral colony, digesting tissue as it

68

67: This nudibranch needs no shell for protection. Having developed tolerance to the orange sponge's toxic defensive chemicals, it feeds on the sponge, steals the chemicals, and stores them for its own protection. (*Reticulidia fungia*, Fiji)
68: In addition to using a sponge's chemical protective system, some flatworms (*Pseudoceros dimidiata*) and nudibranchs are brilliantly colored to serve as a warning that they are not good to eat. (Fiji)

advances, and leaving behind a white skeleton. The black band is an advancing front of these organisms causing coral death. It is likely that stressed corals are more vulnerable to this disease but very little is known about the details of this process (*41*). (Plate 69)

White-band disease also results in tissue death, and the white color is due to the loss of coral tissue and the exposed white skeleton. No one knows whether this disease is a pathogen or whether some other factor is responsible, since corals are vulnerable to infections from bacteria and other pathogens (*42*).

These are only two of 30 diseases that infect corals. Although the specific causes of most remain a mystery, bacteria, fungi, algae, worms, and general stress can also cause coral disease. A global database has shown that 97 percent of sites where coral disease has been observed correlates with human activity. Some estimates suggest that 80 percent of corals in the Caribbean have been lost to disease from the 1980s to early 2000 (*43*). Whether it be a human body or an ecosystem like a coral reef, it seems clear that the greater the number of environmental insults

69: This brain coral (*Diploria labyrinthiformis*) is being attacked by the black-band disease. The white area is dead coral where no tissue remains, having been digested by the black-band disease. Note the space separating the larger coral from its neighbor, lower center, indicating a no-man's-land where the two colonies have competed for space. (Caribbean)

70

or organisms an ecosystem must face, the more likely it is to be susceptible to disease.

Finally, there is coral bleaching, which is a natural phenomena; yet, it can result in coral death. For instance, corals may eject their zooxanthellae (algae), and when they do so they appear "bleached" because coral tissue is clear and the coral skeleton below is white. So, without zooxanthellae and associated pigments, the coral appears white or "bleached." One explanation for why corals may naturally evict their gardens of algae is that it may be a way of replacing an old crop of food producers for a new one, which may have different nutritional qualities or tolerances to environmental conditions and be better adapted to new environmental conditions (*44*). A more serious situation occurs when corals are stressed; in this event they may also eject their gardens of algae. If this lasts for more than a couple of weeks, the corals may die, since they are dependent on their algal partners for food. Massive coral bleaching can result from a number of causes, including but not limited to changes in salinity, increased ultraviolet light, and warmer water temperatures. For instance, global warm-

70: When stressed, corals may lose their symbiotic algae. With the loss of algae and related pigments, the white coral skeleton below can be seen, thus the term coral bleaching. But many corals create their own pigments that become apparent after the algae have gone, seen in the purple areas of this staghorn coral (*Acropora* sp., Fiji).
71: The purple, pink, and yellow colors of corals involved in the process of bleaching indicate pigments not associated with the symbiotic algae. These pigments may be used as antennae to collect more sunlight for photosynthesis and/or as sunblocks for protection from too much sun. Although beautiful, this table coral is in the process of dying. (*Acropora* sp., Fiji)

ing is already stressing many coral species living near their upper temperature limit for warm water and causing massive bleaching—as was seen during the 1982–83 and 1997–98 El Niño warming events. Unlike the 1982–83 El Niño, which primarily impacted reefs along the west coast of North, Central, and South America, the 1997–98 episode affected reefs in the Indian Ocean, southeast and east Asia, the Pacific Ocean, the Caribbean, and the Atlantic Ocean. The latter El Niño episode destroyed about 16 percent of the corals on reefs of the world in nine months.

There is now general consensus that climate change and global warming are causing frequent warming periods and that these events are certain to increase in the future. Traditionally conservative reef scientists are predicting that many reefs are doomed due to global warming (*45*). (Plates 70, 71)

In addition to threats related to diseases and rising water temperatures, reefs are subject to plagues. Plagues are caused by a disease or invading species that sweeps through a population with devastating consequences. As with coral disease the occurrence of these plagues seems to be on the rise and related to human influences. The crown-of-thorns plague, for instance, appears to be related to disruption of landscapes and release of nutrients to coastal waters (*46*). The population explosions of these sea stars can kill corals on a massive scale. The sea stars evert their stomachs to digest and assimilate coral tissue, leaving behind a white skeleton. Now the evidence seems to indicate that nutrient enrichment of coastal waters provides more food for the larval starfish, thus enabling more of them to survive to adulthood. It has been suggested that the loss of triton shells and large groupers, both known predators of the crown-of-thorns, may enable more of the young to survive and eventually overwhelm reefs. But, historically, their populations have been so low that their effectiveness as controlling agents seems unlikely. Crown-of-thorns sea stars have been around for millions of years and thus are a natural part of the reef ecosystem, so it's not the presence of the species that is a problem but how abundant it is.

72: This coral (*Acropora* sp.) has recently been preyed upon by the crown-of-thorns sea star (*Acanthaster planci*). The white skeleton is exposed after the coral's tissue has been digested by the predator. (Fiji)

73: Once dead, from whatever cause, coral skeletons are rapidly colonized by algae. In this case, a table coral skeleton has been taken over by filamentous blue-green algae (cyanophytes). (Fiji)

The crown-of-thorns issue has been controversial because there is little solid historical evidence about past crown-of-thorns plagues (*47*). Whether these sea stars are good or bad for the reef may depend on how frequently their populations explode into a plague. Forest fires are a good example of this question. They may be considered good if they occur infrequently, but may be considered detrimental if they rage through a forest so often that the forest doesn't have a chance to recover, causing the ecosystem to deteriorate. This matter is still under investigation and the debate continues. (Plate 72)

The most dramatic plague ever seen on coral reefs was the massive die-off in 1983 of *Diadema antillarum* sea urchins in the Caribbean, where crown-of-thorns starfish are not found. An epidemic swept from Panama to Bermuda in 13 months, resulting in the death of perhaps 100 percent of the urchins on some reefs and more than a 95 percent mortality throughout the Caribbean (*48*). The ecological consequences of this mass mortality were almost as dramatic. The demise of these herbivores, which kept much of the algal growth in check, resulted in increases in algae by as much as 439 percent (*49*). This, in turn, smothered corals and covered exposed bottom areas required by coral larvae for settling and building new colonies. The sudden absence of these lawn mowers and the wide range of ecological consequences dramatized how inter-related species are in the coral city. Everything *is* connected!

Pollution

In the Caribbean the loss of herbivores has been exacerbated by pollution. We generally think of a pollutant as a toxic chemical that upsets an important physiological metabolic process, causing illness, but nutrient enrichment can also act as pollution because it alters the environmental conditions important to corals. (Plate 73) This is because reefs exist as oases in the biological desert of the open sea. Instead of lacking water, the oceanic deserts lack appreciable quantities of nutrients—nitrogen and phosphorus, which fertilize plants or algae. Irrigating a desert benefits species better equipped to survive in an environment with more water; as a consequence, plants and animals adapted to drought suffer. In the case of reefs, adding excessive amounts of nutrients causes a variety of changes in the ecosystem, most of which are not good for corals. Too many nutrients give algae an advantage over corals, thus enabling algae to overgrow corals or cover surfaces where coral larvae might settle and form new colonies. Excess nutrients can upset the balance between corals and their zooxanthellae, causing algae to divert the food they produce to reproduction, rather than releasing it to corals (*50*). Some nutrients reduce the coral's ability to construct its skeleton (*51*). Finally, increases in nutrients promote the growth of boring sponges, bivalves, and micro-organisms that erode the reef (*52*). As with most pollutants, a little is not necessarily bad, but too much can be catastrophic.

Generally, we have considered the nutrient enrichment problem to be a relatively local or regional problem, but recent research has changed that assumption. The scale of nutrient enrichment of reefs is becoming vast. We know that human population growth has resulted in forest destruction on an unprecedented scale, with resultant erosion and nutrient runoff. More farms have been created and fertilized, and more sewage released into coastal waters.

A global shift in weather patterns, which took place from 1972 to 1976, caused a reduction in Sahara rainfall and thus an increase in dust transported to the western Atlantic by high altitude winds. Satellite imagery and on-site studies have confirmed that hundreds of millions of tons of African dust are carried annually to the Caribbean region and the Americas (*53*). (Plate 74) It appears likely that this dust, like all dust, contains nutrients, particularly iron, which not only can fertilize algae living on reefs but can also fertilize blue-green algae (*Trichodesmium* sp.) living in open water. These blue-green algae are capable of fixing nitrogen from the atmosphere. So,

74: Algae of a variety of species have taken over this coral and are likely to prevent future coral larvae from settling and rebuilding the reef. (Caribbean)

75

with more iron more bacteria can fix more nitrogen, which is added to already high nitrogen levels on reefs coming from the Sahara dust directly (*54*). There is some speculation that the increase in coral diseases and the devastating *Diadema* sea-urchin disease may be related to this nutrient-bacteria connection. At the moment, the evidence is largely circumstantial, but the fact that what is happening in the Sahara is connected to Caribbean reefs shows how inextricably linked are all places and activities on our planet. (Plate 75)

Although the shift in Saharan weather patterns may be a totally natural phenomenon, the increase in atmospheric carbon dioxide is not. During the last thousand years, humans have begun to burn fossil fuels, disturbing the natural ecology of the planet and raising the concentration of CO_2 by 25 percent, from 279 parts per million to 368 parts per million. This is the highest level in the last 420,000 years (*55*). Presently, it is rising one-half of one percent per year. We know that carbon dioxide is a greenhouse gas and is contributing to global warming. We also know that higher temperatures possibly caused by global warming are causing corals to bleach and die worldwide.

75: A contributing factor in the widespread death of Caribbean corals may be nutrient enrichment linked to dust from the Sahara Desert. (Caribbean)
76: Scientists study the optical characteristics of healthy and unhealthy corals to provide "ground-truth" data that will help in monitoring reefs from high altitude remote sensors placed on planes and satellites. (Fiji)

But CO_2 can also affect reefs directly. Increases in CO_2 alter the carbonate chemistry of seawater and cause a decline in corals' ability to create their calcium carbonate skeletons. In addition, recent studies have shown that small increases in CO_2 can inhibit photosynthesis in the zooxanthellae that coral depend on for food, and cause coral bleaching, even without a rise in temperature. A study by Dr. Martin Pêcheux concluded that a future rise in CO_2 levels will have an effect comparable to a rise in temperature of 2.8°C to 4.5°C in addition to global warming (*56*). The author concluded, "I surmise that reefs as they are known today will disappear. Reef scientists must urgently call for a strong mitigation of anthropogenic (coming from human activities) CO_2." So, changes in atmospheric CO_2 not only cause greenhouse warming and resultant coral bleaching and death but CO_2 can also reduce corals' ability to restore and rebuild reefs!

Scientists have been at a loss to arrive at definitive answers or to explain why, over the last ten or twenty years, reefs damaged by a variety of causes have shown little or no recovery. Whatever the reasons, from the perspective of planetary health, coral reefs may be like canaries in a mine serving as sensitive indicators of environmental health. Reefs may be warning us by their sickness of some serious global problems, problems caused by humans and problems that can only be solved by humans. (Plate 76)

76

CHAPTER FIVE
Conflict and Cooperation

STAYING ALIVE IS the name of the game in any city, and survival involves many ways to protect oneself from danger. In human communities, some of us learn karate, hire a bodyguard, carry mace, or live behind walls. In the coral city all of these same strategies are used, and more.

Competition

For some corals, danger comes in the form of neighbors competing for a place in the sun. Reef-building corals need sunlight for their algal partners; thus, one coral shading another or growing over it may mean death for the loser. These silent warriors employ a variety of strategies for staying alive. Species like staghorn and elkhorn corals grow fast and rise above the competition. (Plate 77) Some merely overgrow their neighbors, and some of the more massive and slower-growing corals actively do battle with their neighbors, using long digestive filaments or special tentacles to sting and dissolve the tissues of competitors. Within these fighting species is a complex system of hierarchy, where species A may kill species B, which in turn dominates species C. But species C may be able to kill species A (57). So, it pays to pick your neighbors! (This complex hierarchy of interactions has been identified in the Caribbean but in the Indo-Pacific it is less well defined.) (Plates 78, 79)

The zones where competing corals have met, done battle, and withdrawn can be identified by a demilitarized zone (DMZ) or no-man's-land. This is an obvious space where neither coral ventures, having concluded that further conflict is not worth the cost.

78

77: In the struggle for space and light, a table coral (*Acropora hyacinthus*) has grown completely around a staghorn coral (*Acropora* sp.). (Fiji)

78 and 79: In their silent wars, one coral may grow over a neighbor of the same species (*Diploria strigosa*) while others may fight by extending tentacles or digestive filaments to kill or ward off an opponent (*Diploria strigosa*, above; *Montrastrea cavernosa*, below). The zone of conflict is indicated by the space between the two coral colonies. (Fiji)

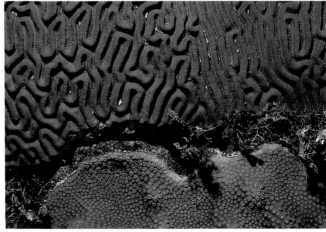

79

The width of the DMZ reflects the distance to which the tentacles or filaments exert their effects.

On a more dramatic scale, fish are also territorial, ready to fight to protect their home, nesting site, or source of food. Remember the gardener damselfish attacking its reflection in the mirror and protecting its garden of algae from intruders in Chapter One? This image of the fish attacking the mirror demonstrates the seriousness with which the fish takes the intrusion, but the actual attack is the culmination of a series of threatening behaviors. Many territorial damselfish attempt to deter an intruder with a series of quick darts and a raised dorsal fin to indicate that the owner of that territory is perturbed. Some species make chirps or grunts. If this doesn't work, the damselfish may attack, biting other fish and even a diver many times its size.

Some fish called grunts threaten with open, reddish mouths when competing with others of their species. (Plate 80) A grouper is particularly vulnerable to human spearfishers, because it may stand its ground when a diver approaches its home range, thus making the

80: Bright red mouths of bluestriped grunts likely enhance their threatening gestures as they do battle. (*Haemulon sciurus*, Caribbean)

fish an easy target. Some surgeonfish use their razor sharp spines in fighting, as a tactic that can be observed when one closes in on its reflection in a mirror and flicks the glass with its spine.

Creative Protection—Simple Stingers

Imagine you are walking through the inner city. You are alone, not particularly big, and not particularly tough. But you feel "ten-feet tall and bullet-proof" with a can of mace in each hand. Or maybe you have a pit bull lashed to each arm. With such protection you're ready for almost anything or at least you're prepared to ward off an attack with these deterrents and, if nothing else, to buy a little time to flee from danger.

81

82

The boxer crab in the Indo-Pacific uses a similar strategy. These crabs hold an anemone in each pincer. When molested they thrust out their anemones just as a boxer puts up his fists. Tentacles of the anemones contain stinging capsules, so an adversary is met with the crab's bodyguards, a "fistfull" of anemones, each armed with chemical defenses. (Plate 81)

81: With its two-fisted defense of sea anemones, this boxer crab relies on both chemical protection from the stinging tentacles and mechanical protection from its exoskeleton. (*Lybia* sp., Fiji)

82: This sponge crab has hind legs adapted to hold its sponge, bodyguard close. Presumably the toxic sponge deters predators from eating the crab. (*Dromidiopsis edwardsi*, Fiji)

Less dramatic but equally effective is the strategy used by the sponge crab. Instead of a toxic defender in each pincer, sponge crabs wear a protective hat. They snip off pieces of a living sponge, presumably inedible or toxic, and tailor them to the contour of their shells, using specially adapted hind legs to hold them tight to the shell, in some cases until the sponge adheres on its own. (Plate 82)

Anyone who has brushed against a piece of fire coral or jellyfish appreciates the effectiveness of their stinging capsules. Tentacles of these animals contain ingenious devices called nematocysts, which are tiny capsules in which threads are coiled, ready for action. (Figure 3) (Plates 83, 84) Upon discharge, the threads shoot out, acting as harpoons to impale and immobilize a victim. Some are able to inject venom, a chemical that gives us the sensation of stinging and serves to paralyze the victim. Nematocysts are sensitive to both chemicals and to touch and are powered by hydraulic pressure. For example, when touched, the nematocyst's capsule is flooded with water. The resultant increase in pressure triggers a reaction that forces the harpoon out and into the victim. Remaining attached to the tentacle, the thread helps insure that the prey won't wiggle free before the venom takes effect. The venom, for the most part, is intended for subduing tiny crustaceans, fish, and other prey,

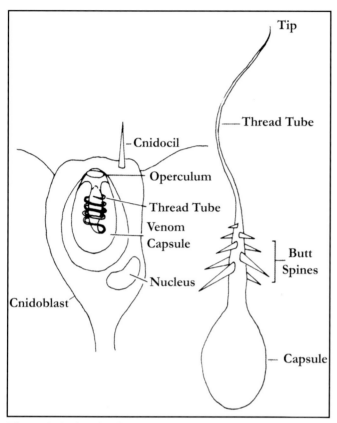

Figure 3. A sketch of the nematocyst of the jellyfish *Physalia*. (From Halstead, *Poisonous and Venomous Marine Animals of the World*. Artist: R. Kreuzinger)

83

84

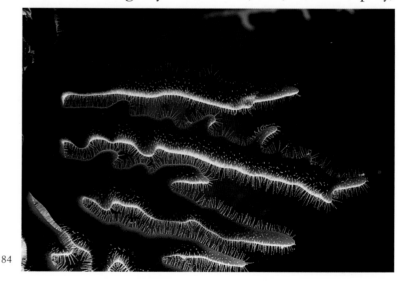

and is quite powerful in some species of anemones and jellyfish. But some venom is incredibly potent: A person can die in a matter of minutes if stung by the deadly sea wasp jellyfish (*Chironex fleckeri*) of northeastern Australia.

Almost all members of the group of animals of which corals and jellyfish are members (Phylum Cnidaria) possess stinging capsules. This phylum includes corals and anemones (Anthozoa), jellyfishes (Scyphozoa), and the hydroids and fire corals (Hydrozoa), which include their open-ocean relatives such as the Portuguese Man-O-War, whose venom is particularly strong. Cnidarians have been around for at least 600 million years, and thus it is not surprising that other animals on the reef have formed alliances with these stingers for their own benefit and in some cases for the benefit of both parties. (Plates 85, 86)

Caribbean corkscrew anemones, for example, are home to a number of crustaceans, such as the Pederson cleaner shrimp, red snapping shrimp, and mysid shrimp. The Pederson cleaner shrimp sit near the anemone and wave their antennae to attract the attention of patients. Some of these shrimp are either so hungry and

86

85

83 and 84: Fire coral derives its name from a burning sensation when one touches it. When illuminated from a different angle, the stinging tentacles become visible. Imbedded in the tentacles are microscopic nematocysts that can shoot out a thread and inject a potent venom designed to paralyze a victim or deter a predator. (*Millepora alcicornis*, Caribbean) 85 and 86: Groups of nematocysts give tentacles of these corals a textured surface. Seen at night, they have their tentacles fully extended to feed on zooplankton that emerges from the reef after dark. Dendrophyllid coral, (Palau)

87: A Pederson cleaner shrimp sits in front of its home anemone (right), immune to the stinging tentacles. It rocks back and forth while waving its antennae to attract fish for cleaning. (*Periclimenes pedersoni*, Caribbean)

88: A snapping shrimp, or pistol shrimp, has been teased out of its home anemone. The enlarged pincer is used to make a loud pop that has sufficient force to either stun a meal or ward off a predator. (*Alpheus armatus*, Caribbean)

bold or so curious that they will venture on to a diver's hand and actually clean it. The sensation is that of gentle pin pricks. Being immune to the sting of the nematocysts, the shrimp withdraw into the protective tentacles of the anemone when they are threatened. (Plate 87)

The red snapping shrimp is a better tenant but not as friendly. When an intruder approaches the corkscrew anemone, the snapping shrimp's red-and-white antennae emerge. (Plate 88) After deciding the threat is real, the shrimp extends its enlarged pincer, gives a loud snap and then quickly withdraws—presumably providing a degree of protection for both itself and its landlord. Surprisingly, the loud snap is not made by the jaws of the pincers slamming shut but rather by a bubble that is created upon their impact. This bubble is really an empty space, called a cavitation. When it collapses, water moves in to fill the space and impacts itself, causing a loud sound like the pop of a breaking light bulb (*58*). The concussion of the snap is so powerful that it can be used to stun a passing meal, possibly a larval fish or small worm. It is equally effective for defense. Being "snapped" feels like receiving a tiny electric shock. These shrimp are also called pistol shrimp for obvious reasons. They create the cacophony of clicking sounds, like static on a radio, that divers hear in tropical and temperate reefs.

Creative Protection—Complex Harpooners

Like the nematocysts in anemones that contain harpoons to impale, immobilize, and then haul in their prey, cone snails also use harpoons. Most snails have a rough tongue-like organ covered with sharp teeth, called a radula, used to scrape algae from the ocean bottom. Some of these snails are bio-eroders, slowly excavating bits of reef and contributing to the intertidal notch of limestone shorelines, discussed in Chapter Three. In cone snails, the teeth are rolled into a hollow tubelike structure that serves as a dart that can be thrust into prey (*59*). Like the nematocysts, each harpoon is propelled by hydraulic pressure, but in this case the pressure is created by the muscular contraction of a water-filled chamber. The shaft of the tooth is filled with a venom immediately prior to discharge and entry into the flesh of the victim. (Figure 4)

Cone snails can be divided into three groups according to whether they eat fish, molluscs, or worms. The venom of each group is chemically adapted to their prey. Of these prey categories, humans are most closely related to fish, and thus fish-eating cone snails are the most dangerous to us. People stung by fish-eating cone snails, such as textile cones, have died, which is another reason for not collecting live shells. Another aspect is the requirement for a fast-acting venom. In order to have a relatively sluggish snail catch a very mobile fish, the snail's venom must immobilize the fish before it flees. Often the potential meal that has been harpooned is too large to bring into the shell for digestion. In such cases, a snail may evert its mouth far outside the body and simply engulf the meal for slow digestion outside the stomach proper. (Plates 89, 90)

Conotoxins are the name of the chemicals produced by these snails. Their effects are varied, acting on a remarkable variety of processes associated with nerve function, but the bottom line is that

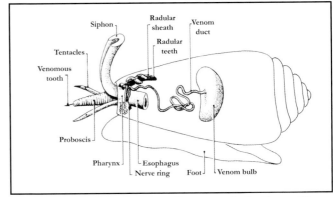

Figure 4. Venom apparatus of a cone shell, *Conus.* (From Halstead, *Poisonous and Venomous Marine Animals of the World.* Artist: R. H. Knabenbauer)

89 and 90: Cone snails have a venomous harpoon used to impale and paralyze a meal. If the prey is too large to "swallow," the mouth can be everted to engulf the meal. (*Conus* sp., Palau)

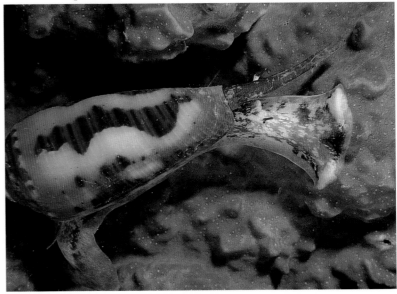

they cause paralysis. The peptide compounds from cone-snail venom have been the source of an important new suite of drugs that block specific nerve action related to pain (*60*). One drug, called Ziconotide, which is produced by the Elan Corporation, is the ultimate pain reliever for terminally-ill people with chronic intractable pain. This new drug has advantages over opioids in that it does not lose potency over time nor is there development of tolerance to it. Some of the wonders of the reef armamentarium actually are of great benefit to humankind.

Better Living through Chemistry

The fact that you can see an alga on the reef indicates that it has some kind of chemical or mechanical deterrent to protect it from the onslaught of grazing herbivorous lawnmowers; otherwise it would be grazed down to being almost invisible (*61*). Like the sponges, algae create chemicals that are distasteful or even poisonous, but some are designed for a different effect. They take the approach of Tums or Maalox to the extreme. Too much antacid can create problems. Most animals use acid to break down their food; without acid, therefore, digestion is impeded. No acid, no digestion.

An example is the green segmented algae of the genus *Halimeda*, seen on most reefs. It not only uses distasteful chemicals to deter predators but it also impregnates its tissues with calcium carbonate. The calcium carbonate has no nutritional value and serves as a deterrent by causing the ratio of inedible to edible material to shift toward the inedible side, thus making it not worth the effort to consume the algae. In addition, the calcium carbonate has been shown to act as an acid neutralizer (*62*). So, any fish grazing on segments of *Halimeda* will not only get a lot of inedible calcium carbonate but will also have their digestive processes disrupted. In addition, *Halimeda*, uses distasteful chemicals for a final deterrent, as does *Caulerpa*, which is full of chemicals. This multi-pronged ap-

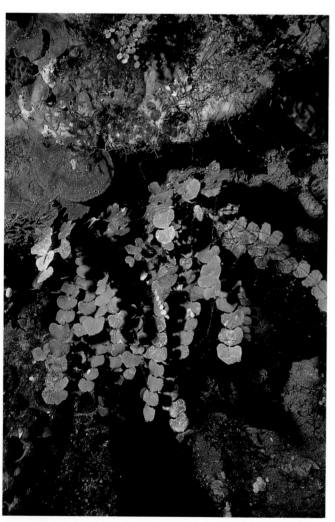

91: These green-segmented algae impregnate their tissue with calcium carbonate and noxious chemicals as an effective deterrent to predators. (*Halimeda* sp., Fiji)

proach covers all the bases: Fish won't get much nutrition from the algae; those relying on acid for digestion will have a problem with digestion; and other fish, such as some parrotfish that don't rely on acid in their digestive process (*63*), will be deterred by the distasteful chemicals. (Plates 91, 92)

There are some animals that, instead of being deterred by these chemical defenses, are attracted to them. The brown alga, *Dictyota bartayresii*, is not only a source of food for a small amphipod, a relative of beach hoppers or sand fleas, but is also home for the amphipod. Since this alga is unpalatable to fish, the little amphipod sets up residence on the alga, folding the fronds over on itself and living inside a chemically protected, edible home (*64*).

In this world of "better living through chemistry" there are endless variations. For example, in a human community no one usually installs an expensive alarm system to protect a home against burglars in a crime-free neighborhood unless you watch big city news too much and are totally paranoid. If there is no danger, then who needs protection?

92: Curiously, distasteful chemicals protect sea grapes (green alga) from fish predation. This alga is commonly eaten by humans in some island cultures. It is a mildly spicy addition to enliven salads. (*Caulerpa recemosa*, Fiji)

93: Although seldom seen during the day, this slipper lobster is protected by its suit of armor (exoskeleton). The price paid for this is that, to grow, the old armor must be shed and a new, larger one constructed. (*Arctides regalis*, Caribbean)

Some coral city residents are also frugal, and don't waste energy in protective chemical systems if they are not needed. Recent studies have shown that some algae, sponges, and even corals possess "inducible defenses," meaning that they produce their protective systems only after they have been grazed or nipped. After being nipped by angelfish, one coral species, *Porites compressa,* fabricates additional stinging capsules and possibly distasteful chemicals (*65*). The angelfish grazing on such corals that have "installed" better defenses immediately withdraws, shaking its head because its mouth has been "zapped" by the reinforced battery of stingers.

Suits of Armor

In our history of armed conflict, the development of armor was a major breakthrough, since it rendered arrows ineffective. Although soldiers were protected, there was a price to be paid in mobility and comfort.

Humans were not the first to use armored protection. Crabs, shrimps, lobsters, and most of their relatives have been using suits of armor for millions of years. They have what is called an exo-

94: Many tropical bivalves live exposed, like this rock oyster, but have extremely thick shells for protection against wrasses and triggerfish that have extremely strong jaws and teeth. (*Spondylus* sp., Fiji)

skeleton. But living and growing inside a rigid encasement presents a challenge. The problem is solved by simply throwing away the old armor and replacing it with a larger set. Although this is an effective strategy, it is costly to build a new suit of armor every so often, and until the new one hardens the individual is effectively naked and vulnerable. (Plate 93)

Molluscs such as bivalves, snails, and chambered nautiluses have protected themselves in shells for at least 600 million years. (Plates 94, 95) The chambered nautilus and its close relatives overcame the weight and mobility restrictions of the heavy shell by filling it with gas to provide buoyancy and freedom from life on the bottom.

95: The chambered nautilus is a resident of deep reefs and compensates for the weight of its shell by filling it with gas to achieve neutral buoyancy. (*Nautilus pompilus*, Palau)

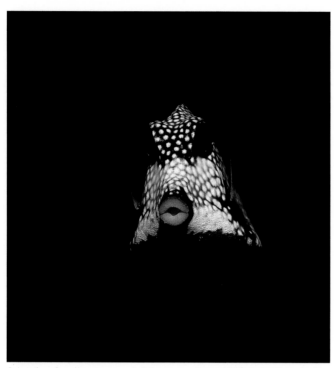

96: The family name of this smooth trunkfish indicates that it is of the family Ostraciidae. The name alludes to the protective, bony encasement created by its fused scales. (*Lactophrys triqueter*, Caribbean)

Even the first fish were heavily protected with armored scales. Called ostracoderms (*ostraco*, bone; *derm*, skin), they lived more than 450 million years ago and gave rise to the sharks and bony fishes. Today we have box-, cow-, and trunkfishes, all of which are encased in a hard covering. Their armor is composed of adjoining bony scales that can grow as the fish grows, avoiding the problem of molting, or shedding, an exoskeleton. (Plate 96) In others, like the spiny puffers, scales have been modified into sharp spines. The scales are folded back most of the time, presumably for stream-lining. But when the puffer is molested it gulps water, causing the skin to be stretched and the spines to become erect. This is really a two-fold defense: Not only do the spines deter a predator, but puffing up makes the fish harder to swallow. (Plate 97)

This evolutionary creativity doesn't stop with physical form; there is chemistry at work as well. Species of the pufferfish family contain a very potent poison called tetrodotoxin, a neurotoxin that is apparently produced by bacteria in the fish's gut. Puffers bred in captivity do not produce the toxin until they are fed the organs of wild fish. There is some evidence that puffer toxin has been part of the concoction used to create zombies, or at least a state of cata-tonic sleep, in some cultures. The Japanese consider puffer a deli-cacy, calling it "fugu." Fugu chefs must attend special classes to be legally certified to work with pufferfish. There are now puffer aqua-culture farms insuring a steady supply of the delicacy; yet, people die every year in Japan from poorly prepared fugu.

Curiously, puffers that can kill may also contribute to pre-serving human lives. The connection lies in the human genome project. We now know that humans have around 30,000 genes (*66*). These genes and associated genetic material include around three billion bases of DNA (letters that make up our genetic alphabet). Remarkably, the genes containing useful information, or at least in-formation that codes for proteins, constitute less than three percent of the total genetic material. This has been a major problem for scientists trying to understand our genetic make up. Less than a three percent return on investment, even when genes are identifiable, is rather poor, especially since the process of identifying the genes and determining the order in which they are arranged on chromosomes is an expensive business.

All of us vertebrates share fundamental early developmental patterns and are more or less physiologically similar. Presumably, it is the way in which genes are regulated, rather than different genes,

97: Spiny pufferfish have taken protection to the extreme. Their tissue is poisonous; they can gulp water to make themselves too big to eat by most predators; and they have modified their scales into spines that are erected when the body inflates. (*Cyclichthys antillarum*, Caribbean)

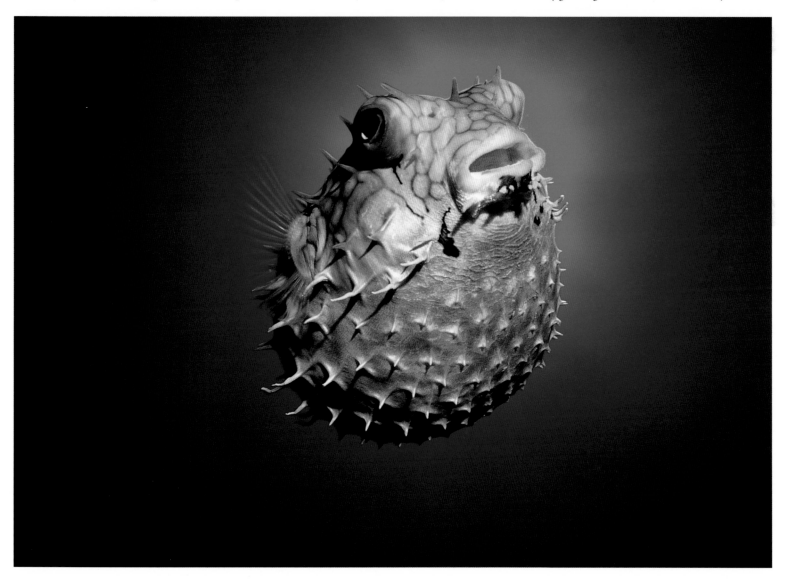

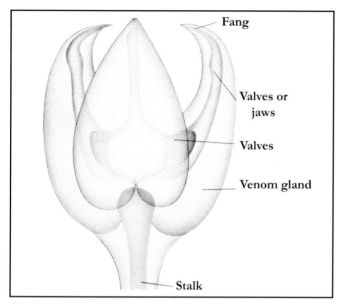

Figure 5. Structure of a venemous sea urchin globiferous pedicellarium from the test, or shell. (From Halstead, *Poisonous and Venomous Marine Animals of the World.* Artist: R. Kreuzinger, after Mortensen)

98: The thin spines of many sea urchins are designed to easily penetrate skin and break off, leaving a painful wound. (*Echinostrephus* sp., Papua New Guinea)

99: Thick spines of pencil urchins may be too much trouble for predatory fish to munch through. (*Heterocentrotus mammillatus*, Hawaii)

100: Sea urchins that have almost no spines are not without defenses. Tiny pincers, pedicellariae, with red centers cover the body, ready to clamp down and inject a toxic venom into any intruder making contact. (*Toxopneustes pileolus*, Papua New Guinea)

that give rise to vertebrate diversity. Thus, one would expect that all vertebrates have a similar repertoire of genes, due to the way in which genomes have evolved. It has been observed that the more "primitive" the vertebrate, the smaller its genome and thus the percentage of "useful" genetic material would be expected to be much higher than in humans. Studies have shown that pufferfish have about the same number of genes as do humans; but they have a smaller genome (smaller amount of DNA) because it is a fish and thus a more simple vertebrate. Work has been underway to sequence the puffer genome and then compare the "useful" portions to that of humans in hope of helping us focus on the "important" sections of our genome and helping us ignore what some call "junk DNA" (*67*).

Echinoderms are the master of spines, as their name suggests (*echino*, spine; *derm*, skin), and sea urchins are among the spiniest of the group. But not all spines are created equal. Long skinny spines are an effective defense because they easily penetrate the skin and they hurt, but what about the thick spines of pencil urchins found in coral crevices? Researchers have suggested that these spines resist the tough jaws of triggerfish, making it harder for them to chew down through the spines to the body of the urchin. Even stranger are urchins that have almost no spines at all. These urchins, as do so many creatures discussed in this chapter, rely on "better living through chemistry." Most urchins and some sea stars have tiny pincers called pedicellariae, which contain venom. (Figure 5) This venom is a neurotoxin and in some urchins can cause respiratory problems in humans (*68*). So, this seemingly defenseless creature may harbor the greatest threat if handled. (Plate 98, 99, 100)

Strategies for Survival

As we conclude this chapter on conflict and cooperation, I am reminded of the many variations on these themes. In nature there is no right or wrong way to survive. Although defensive and

98

99

100

offensive strategies are extremely varied, employing effective strategies is absolutely essential in a species fulfilling its evolutionary mandate—to stay alive long enough to reproduce and perpetuate the species and most importantly to transmit its genes to the next generation. Those strategies for survival range from the shape and physical adaptations of a species to its physiological tolerances and to behavioral traits and relationships.

Consider the physical adaptations of triggerfish whose name comes from the defensive modification of the dorsal spine. Behind and under this spine is a bone that can be raised to prop it up. When both are erected the spine cannot be lowered, thus making the fish much more difficult to swallow. Only when the lower bone is depressed, i.e., when the trigger is pulled back, can the spine be lowered. Triggerfish, and many reef fish, have laterally compressed bodies, whereby they are very thin from side to side but elongated top to bottom. Presumably this makes them harder to swallow. Watching a moray eel struggling to consume a reef fish with such a shape certainly suggests that shape does offer some benefit.

I was reminded of how behavioral adaptations can be of benefit while diving the reefs of San Salvador Island in the Bahamas some years back. I noticed a queen triggerfish approaching and realized it had a companion, a bar jack. I had not seen this association before and wondered what was going on. It did not take long for the reason to be obvious. Triggerfish feed on invertebrates such as sea urchins, crabs, and other shellfish; they do not feed on fish. Consequently, small reef fish ignore an approaching triggerfish. On the other hand, bar jacks are voracious predators on small reef fish. I remained still, took a picture, and waited for my strobe to recycle. Suddenly before my eyes the bar jack, which had been on the open-water side of the triggerfish, darted to the reef and grabbed an unsuspecting victim. The strategy was obvious, the triggerfish would not cause alarm in small fish since they were not its prey items. By hiding behind its companion and using it as a decoy the bar jack could get better access to a meal than if it were swimming alone and thus visible to potential prey. (Plate 101)

This was a good example of commensalism, defined as a relationship where one member benefits while the other is neither helped nor harmed. The triggerfish was oblivious to the jack while the jack was definitely helped in its feeding by associating with the triggerfish. Divers often see jacks and other fish hovering next to rays as they cruise over the bottom, excavating it for crustaceans and shellfish. As other creatures are disturbed and flee, the commensal freeloaders dart in for an easy meal (*69*).

101: A bar jack (*Carans ruber*) swims with a queen trigger, on the side away from the reef, using it as a decoy. Since the queen trigger (*Balistes vetula*) feeds on invertebrates and the jack preys on fish, the jack can get closer to unsuspecting fish by hiding next to the trigger. Immediately after this photo was taken, the jack darted to the reef and grabbed a very surprised fish. (Caribbean)

The larger category into which commensalism falls is symbiosis, which refers to individuals of two species living together or interacting in some way. There are two other subsets of symbiosis. At one extreme is mutualism, where both partners benefit from the relationship, such as corals and zooxanthellae or the boxer crab and its partner anemones. At the other extreme is parasitism, where one species benefits at the expense of the other, such as the isopods and other disease organisms that infect fish and are removed by reef cleaners.

All of these stories reflect the incredible evolutionary creativity and adaptations by which species meet the challenges of survival. (Plate 102) Yet, even as we live in what some might call our human, "artificial communities," we are not outside the fundamental evolutionary imperative to survive and procreate. And our strategies for survival include many of the same approaches discussed for the coral city. We compete for space, using chemical warfare and employing armor for protection. We appropriate chemicals from other species to protect us from invading disease. We use other species to guard our property and ourselves. And we form all sorts of symbiotic relationships with friends, family, loved ones, or business associates and partners, ranging from parasitic relationships and shady practices to the mutualistic partnerships in our personal and professional lives that are ultimately the foundation of all good relationships.

102: In the reef's web of life everything is connected and nothing exists alone. These yellowfin goatfish seek refuge in a reef cave and feed on crustaceans living in sand. Some of the sand was likely created by parrotfish and sea urchins, which, through their feeding, may have helped excavate the reef to create the cave where the goatfish now hide. (*Mulloides venicolensis*, Fiji)

CHAPTER SIX
Advertising

AS THE PACE OF LIFE in cities increases, communication often becomes reduced to condensed, highly visible messages. This is especially true in advertising, where simple visual symbols are designed to catch the eye and convey a clear and unmistakable message.

In the coral city, relatively simple animals communicate simple messages. Many of these messages have critical life or death implications relating to protecting home or nest, mating, and avoiding being eaten. With so much at stake, it is essential that the messages be unambiguous. Consequently, these animals are advertising with dramatic gestures and colorful symbols.

Health Benefits and Beneficiaries

There are many species of health practitioners on the reef, and some of them have evolutionarily converged in their advertising. Gobies and wrasses have similar coloration to identify them as cleaners, with lateral lines of blue and black color (70). A common coloration among different species that perform the same job is presumably beneficial to all. It reinforces the message, making it easier for other species to learn who are cleaners and who are not. The barber shrimp, on the other hand, uses color as an undersea Red Cross, signifying that it should not be harmed because of the important health services it performs. (Plate 103) These dramatic colors presumably attract patients and protect it from predation.

103: Serving the same purpose as a red and white barber pole, the colors of this barber shrimp advertise to attract customers to be cleaned. (*Stenopus hispidus*, Caribbean)

The advertising of cleaners is not limited to color coding (Plate 104) but can sometimes involve behavior as well. Some juvenile cleaner wrasses of the genus *Labroides* attract customers by swimming in a rhythmic fashion with their tails bobbing up and down. Similarly, the Pederson cleaner shrimp, which lives in association with the corkscrew anemone, advertises by rocking back and forth while fluttering its white antennae.

Patients also advertise their interest in being cleaned. Creole wrasses of the Caribbean orient themselves in a head-down position to let cleaners know they are ready to be serviced, as do parrotfishes and some jacks. (Plate 105) Some goatfish extend their chin-whiskers (barbels) and change to a pinkish color when they want to be cleaned. Another possible reason that fish change color may be that parasites adapted to a certain color of the fish may be easier seen by cleaners when the background color changes (*71*).

Danger—Watch Out!

Traffic signals, stop signs, poisons, and hazardous materials are all denoted with an easily recognizable symbol. Similar warning signs exist in the coral city. Many animals having venomous spines, poisons, or distasteful chemicals are brightly colored, often red or yellow. Such warnings, obviously, protect the animal but also protect predators from making a life-threatening mistake by preying on something that could be lethal (*72*).

Many dorid nudibranchs, which are naked snails with a tuft of gills at the stern, store in their bodies noxious chemicals from the sponges and tunicates they eat, thus appropriating another's defense. In some cases, their brilliant colors may even have been stolen from their prey. Some aeolid nudibranchs, which have rows of gills along their dorsal surfaces, also steal defenses from others and advertise with brilliant colors the fact that they are inedible. These nudibranchs eat hydroids, which are relatives of anemones and corals,

104

105

104: Yellow, blue, and black colors identify and advertise this wrasse (*Labroides dimidiatus*) as a cleaner helping it attract "business" from a surgeonfish (*Ctenochetus strigosus*) and avoid being preyed upon . . . it's not good to eat your doctor. (Fiji)

105: By standing on the heads, Creole wrasse identify themselves as patients to be cleaned. (*Clepticus parrae*, Caribbean)

and, like most cnidarians, have stinging capsules—nematocysts. The nudibranchs then incorporate nematocysts from their prey in their gills, and are ready for action if something decides to eat them— quite an ingenious defensive strategy. The nudibranch must eat another critter that already has an effective stinging defensive system and at the same time prevent the stingers from discharging, and then transport them to the nudibranch's gills, storing them without their being discharged and ready for use when needed (*73*). (Plates 106, 107, 108) Even snails with protective shells have evolved to benefit from the defensive systems of their prey. Flamingo tongue snails sport a colorful mantle—a warning that their stolen chemicals make them taste as bad as the sea fans and gorgonians on which they feed (*74*). (Plate 109)

Some fish are much more specific in advertising what to watch out for. For example, surgeonfish are herbivores that help mow the lawn of the reef, but they have a razor-sharp spine sometimes called a scalpel; thus the name surgeonfish. The coloration of many

106: This dorid nudibranch feeds on sponges and stores their toxic chemicals in its body for protection. Beautiful colors advertise that it is not good to eat. (*Chromodoris kunei*, Fiji)
107: Aeolid nudibranchs feed on hydroids and store the stinging capsules (nematocysts) for their own protection. (*Flabellina rubrollineata*, Fiji)
108: Having stolen its defense, this nudibranch uses brilliant colors to warn potential predators that it can sting like a hydroid. (*Cuthona fibogae*, Fiji)
109: Flamingo tongue snails (*Cyphoma gibbosum*) feed on sea fans (*Gorgonia ventalina*) and incorporate their defensive chemicals in the tongue snail's shell mantle. Note the trail where the snail may have been feeding. (Caribbean)

107

108

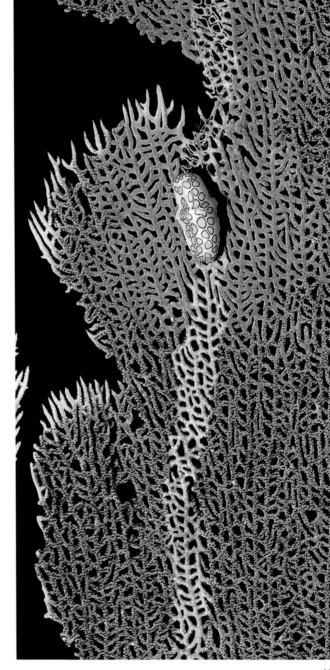

109

110

110: The red colors of this Achilles tang focus attention on the razor sharp spine (scalpel) at the base of its tail. (*Acanthurus achilles*, Society Islands)

111: The white scalpel of this eye-stripe surgeon fish is hinged in such a way as to hook and slash a predator as it passes from the front to the back of the surgeon fish. Notice the cleaner hovering below. (*Acanthurus dussumieri*, Fiji)

111

surgeonfish effectively draws attention to their razor-sharp spine. (Plates 110, 111)

Most worms that crawl about the reef hide in crevices and rubble, but one reddish-colored worm cruises about in broad daylight seemingly unafraid. The name fireworm is a clue to its defense. It not only looks like fire but it feels like fire! Along its sides are tufts of setae, fine hair-like bristles that can cause an extremely painful sting. Touching one of these worms evokes a dramatic erection of these setae, causing the worm to turn almost white. For a diver the reddish color is a welcome stop sign to avoid contact with this worm. (Plate 112)

Some angelfish and butterflyfish advertise with poster colors. Making themselves more visible to other species helps avoid conflict and territorial fights. Such striking colors and patterns also help reduce the possibility of mistaken identity and mating with the wrong species(75). Many species of butterflyfishes and angelfishes are closely related, and their behavior and body forms are very similar. It is important to avoid mating with the wrong species since viable young may not be produced; it would be a waste of sperm and eggs. One solution to this problem, called character displacement, meaning a change in characteristics in order to more easily distinguish one species from another, results in close relatives possessing very distinctive and different colors and patterns so there is no mistaking each species. (Plate 113)

Deception

Deceptive advertising seems to be about as common as honest publicity. We have already seen that a number of cleaner fish species advertise with a blue and black line along their bodies. Identified as cleaners, they are given a degree of immunity from predators and the opportunity to approach other fish at close range. Such identifying colors, which indicate that a fish is a cleaner, can be used for deceptive purposes. Some blennies also have blue and black col-

112: Along the sides of bristle worms, or fire worms, are tiny hairs that can be erected and are extremely irritating to the skin. (*Hermodice carunculata*, Caribbean)

113: Bright colors of this queen angelfish call attention to it, helping ward off competitors and avoiding it being mistaken for a closely related species during mating. (*Holacanthus ciliaris*, Caribbean)

114

115

114: The characteristic coloration of this wrasse identifies it as a cleaner interested in providing medical services. (*Labroides dimidiatus*, Fiji)

115: The coloration of this false-cleaner blenny is designed to deceive a fish into thinking it is a cleaner wrasse. By mimicking a cleaner it may gain close access in order to bite off a scale or part of a fin from its victim. (*Plagiotremus rhinorhyunchus*, Fiji)

116

oration, but they are not cleaners; they are cheats using false advertising to take advantage of the benefits enjoyed by real cleaners (*76*). The coloration of these false cleaners enables them, as mimics, to gain access to other fish. When a customer allows the presumed cleaner to approach at close range, it receives a vicious nip rather than medical treatment. In a sense these false cleaners are parasites, feeding on scales and fins of their victims. (Plates 114, 115)

Obviously, the number of cheats must be far fewer than true cleaners; otherwise, the resident fish population would avoid all fish resembling cleaners and this could bring down the whole symbiotic cleaning system. In fact, real cleaners do cheat from time to time but such behavior is controlled by retaliation from the patient. Studies have shown that, when a cleanee is inappropriately nipped, the cleaner is punished by an aggressive retaliatory response (*77*).

Another form of false advertising is used by fish that act like fishermen. Equipped with a remarkable, miniature fishing rod, frogfishes advertise with what appears to be a little wiggly worm designed to attract other fish. But the fishing rod and wiggly worm are actually a modified spine of the dorsal fin. The incredible camouflage of frogfishes further enhances the effect because those fish interested in eating the worm are unlikely to realize that the wiggly thing is attached to a lurking predator. (Plate 116) When the victim approaches close enough, the frogfish makes a short lunge forward, opens its cavernous mouth, and sucks in the unsuspecting fish—all in a matter of milliseconds.

False advertising also includes false eyes positioned away from the real eyes, presumably to make it much more difficult for a predator to anticipate a potential victim's next move, giving the intended prey a distinct advantage. In the case of butterflyfish and many other reef residents, a large eye-spot, or ocellus, near the tail is the most obvious feature of the fish's coloration. These are not real eyes but certainly convey the impression of an eye (*78*). (Plate 117) This marking has developed not only in a variety of fish species, but also in terrestrial animals like butterflies, suggesting the evolutionary benefits of such ocelli.

117

118

116: Looking like a yellow sponge, the color, body shape, and behavior of a frogfish make it appear very unfishlike. With a small lure it attracts smaller fish and then gulps them down. (*Antennarius commersoni*, Hawaii)

117: The false eye of this 4-eye butterflyfish may confuse a predator just enough to help it avoid being a meal. (*Chaetodon capistratus*, Caribbean)

118: The adaptive advantage of having a large head is that, when this scorpionfish opens its mouth to catch an unsuspecting victim, a great volume of water is sucked in, pulling the prey along with it. (*Scorpaenopsis* sp., Fiji)

119

119: Not only is the body of a peacock flounder adapted for a hidden life on the bottom but it can change color to match the substrate even as it swims from habitat to habitat. (*Bothus lunatus*, Caribbean)

120: These two cowries demonstrate the benefits of having a mantle that covers the shell. The color and projections of the mantle extended over one cowry provide effective camouflage against predatory fish. (*Cypraea vitellus*, Palau)

121: Decorator crabs snip off pieces of red sponge and attach them to hooks on their shells for camouflage and as a deterrent to predators. (*Pelia mutica*, Caribbean)

Camouflage is a form of false advertising, since the animals' coloration, form, and behavior serve to give the impression that it is something other than what it really is. Members of the scorpionfish family, particularly stonefish, are masters of disguise using color and body form, sometimes including extensions of skin to break up the outline of the fish. They sit almost invisible on reefs waiting for prey and avoiding predators. (Plate 118) Flatfish also employ form and coloration for the same reasons. (Plate 119)

Collectors love cowry shells partly because of their glossy sheen. In the sea, algae and invertebrate larvae settle on all available surfaces thus making most shells a mini-reef inhabited by all sorts of organisms. So how does the cowry keep its shell so clean? The answer is that cowries extend their mantle over the shell, in many cases to make the snail harder to see. The mantle may even have little projections, like that of the scorpionfish, to break up the animal's outline and enhance the camouflage effect. (Plate 120)

We have discussed how some species "steal" the defenses of others, but, in the case of decorator crabs, they go a step further: They use other species to help them become invisible! Some of the most effective are Caribbean decorator crabs, which live on red sponges and attach pieces of that sponge to themselves for camouflage. Similarly, other species of crabs use hydroids, algae, and other organisms as decoration, in order to appear to be what they are not. Many of these crabs have fine hooked hairs on their shells, which make it easier for debris to be attached and held until they actually begin growing on the shell. (Plate 121) In fact, the way in which this defense works proves that it was not we humans who first created Velcro.

Lest one think that residents of the coral city must employ either one or another adaptive strategy, consider the lionfish, a mem-

ber of the scorpionfish family. Lionfish are generally known for their attractive, elaborately developed fins, but much of the time those fins are folded up, and the lionfish sits camouflaged on the reef, waiting for a meal to swim by. When bothered, its long and colorful fins are flared, warning that a potent venom will be injected into anything that approaches too close. In this case, one species uses both types of advertising. Camouflage is false advertising, and warning coloration as a stop sign is honest advertising. Each is used depending on the situation. (Plate 122, 123)

So it seems we are bound by the same laws of nature that apply to the coral city. We are visual creatures and rely heavily on this sense to communicate. In many cases reef creatures and humans both use simple symbols to convey unambiguous messages. And, lest we become too preoccupied with the evils lurking in society, we find that deception and cheating have evolved "naturally," long before we created human societies.

122: Next to the red soft coral is a lionfish (*Dendrochirus zebra*) well camouflaged and waiting to grab a basslet (*Pseudanthias squammipinnis*). (Fiji)

123: When the lionfish is perturbed, camouflage is replaced by a colorful warning coloration and venomous fins are flared. (*Pterois volitans*, Fiji)

122

123

CHAPTER SEVEN
Personal Lives

WHETHER IT BE THE coral city or in a human city, there is no best way to earn a living. In both realms we see an incredible variety of strategies for survival and related adaptations. Beyond the basics of "eat and don't get eaten," there are endless variations on personal lifestyles—how to dress, attract a mate, commit to a relationship, raise a family, and so on.

Consider us as a species: Our human needs are all basically the same, but we are far from homogeneous. In fact, depending on one's cultural perspective, we may appear rather weird in our various behaviors, but a closer look at the coral city reveals that some residents rival or even surpass our human strangeness.

Dress Codes And Colors

Take, for instance, the subject of coloration and how we advertise or communicate through color—the topic we have explored in Chapter Six. In some human societies, it would be possible to look at a person and, just by their dress, know their approximate age. Children dress differently from teenagers and both can be distinguished from an adult by their dress.

So it is with many fish. (Plate 124) Some fish not only dress up, but they *change* clothes. There is a progression of colors through which some damselfish and angelfish pass as they mature. In some cases, the more primitive characteristics are most prominent in early developmental stages. As an individual matures, those traits are replaced by later evolutionary advances. Thus, in some species of damselfishes the juveniles of different species look very similar because they evolved from a common ancestor, but as they mature,

124: As we humans use clothes to send a message, so do the beautiful colors of these chevroned butterfly fish help them communicate. (*Chaetodon trifasciatus*, Fiji)

the characteristics unique to each species become apparent. In other cases, juveniles live in different habitats and have different challenges in staying alive; thus, it would be expected that their body shapes and colors would be different. It is difficult to test such evolutionary processes, and mostly we are left with educated speculation and theories still to be studied. In fact, there is much more we don't know about life and behavior on a reef than what we do. (Plates 125, 126, 127)

Why do some fish change colors within a matter of seconds or minutes? We know that some fish change color to communicate their interest in being cleaned, as part of a mating ritual, or a threat. But, as with this filefish, we have no idea what is going on to

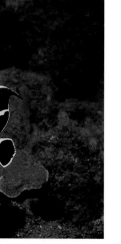  

125   126

125, 126, and 127: Distinctive yellow bars identify a French angelfish as a juvenile. As it matures, the French angel will gradually "change clothes," losing the bars altogether when it reaches adulthood. (*Pomacanthus paru*, Caribbean)

128 and 129: The whitespotted filefish can change its coloration relatively rapidly, but what information is being communicated by this remains a mystery to science. (*Cantherhines macrocerus*, Caribbean)

130 and 131: By altering their color patterns, fish (like this peacock grouper) may communicate readiness to spawn or threaten an intruder in its territory. (*Cephalopholis argus*, Fiji)

cause it to go from its solid color phase to the polka-dot phase. (Plates 128, 129) Likewise, the spotted grouper often changes "clothes," sporting a series of vertical white bars near its tail. (Plates 130, 131)

Sleep

We know that many fish put on their "pajamas" or change from one color phase to another when they sleep at night. In humans the reason is that we want to wear something comfortable to

keep warm while we sleep. But fish are cold-blooded, so warmth is not an issue. It's dark at night, so why would colors make a difference anyway, since they can't be seen? Why would an animal go to the trouble, or invest the energy, to change its coloration? A really convincing explanation has not come from researchers. One speculation is that it may take energy to maintain the daytime colors; at night, when particular colors aren't needed, a fish can relax and just be itself (79). (Plates 132, 133)

Parrotfish go to sleep at night and many change color. But some species of parrotfish take sleeping a step further. They create a sleeping bag out of mucus. Sounds cozy doesn't it—sleeping all rolled up in slime? There are a number of possible reasons for encasing oneself in a sleeping bag. The mucus may prevent noctur-

132

133

132 and 133: In the case of this dash-and-dot goatfish, its coloration at night is more bright than during the day. Why a fish would dress up in gaudy pajamas remains a mystery to science. (*Parupeneus barberinus*, Fiji)

nal predators, like moray eels, from smelling them. The mucus may also serve as a deterrent to parasites lurking on the bottom, waiting to hop aboard a host for a free meal. Research has shown that in the mornings fish have many more parasites, before they have visited a cleaner, than at the end of the day after a number of visits to the reef doctor. So it is clear that night is the time when parasites invade, and thus the sleeping bag may have some protective advantage (*80*). (Plate 134, 135)

Sex Lives

If parrotfish sleeping habits seem strange, their sex lives are even weirder. As with most species of parrotfish, the young hatch from their eggs either as males or as females. But in some species, females can change gender to become males. These sex-changed individuals are called terminal-phase males or super-males. Super-males may look completely different from either females or individuals that began as males, called initial-phase males. Among the most dramatic examples of super-males is the stoplight parrotfish (*81*). Being able to change sex gives the species the ability to adjust male-to-female ratios to maximize each individual's production of young. Since eggs are expensive and sperm is cheap, it is easier for

135

134

134: At night some parrotfish create a "sleeping bag" of mucus, revealed by debris that has settled on the exterior. (*Scarus* sp., Fiji)

135: One possible function of this parrotfish's cocoon (seen as hazy material above the fish) is to deter parasites, which have easy access to fish sleeping on the bottom. (*Scarus ghobban*, Fiji)

a few males to fertilize a greater number of females. Consequently, it is safer to produce more females, and if a shortage of males occurs, some of the females change sex to fill in as needed. (Plates 136, 137)

Since the subject of sex is so emotionally charged, it may be worthwhile to put it in a purely biological perspective before delving into the subject further. Probably because we humans need to give our young so much nurturing and care before they can live on their own, we are programmed to take our parenting duties very seriously, and we get very emotional about the whole process of reproducing. But below all our cooing, cuddling, and proud parenting is the basic obligation to safely store and pass on our genetic material to the next generation, and that's it. Genes, or the information they contain, are somewhat immortal, while the individual as the receptacle and replicator of genes is only transient. Once we have fulfilled our evolutionary role we then self-destruct. Not particularly romantic, but logical. This "selfish-gene" theory does not impose any good, bad, or best on how living things accomplish their job— so long as they do their job (*82*). If they fail, they are a genetic dead end and cease to exist as a species. Nowhere are variations on lifestyles and the theme of reproduction more apparent than in the coral city.

Anemonefishes, also known as clownfishes, are like many others in the damselfish family in that they can be aggressive, protecting their anemone homes from intruders while at the same time protecting their young (*83*). Their adaptations and behaviors are ingenious. Their bodies are coated with mucus, which protects them from the anemone's nematocysts, so they are able to live in a bed of otherwise lethal stingers, protected from predators. This is a mutualistic relationship: Since there are some fish that prey on the anemone's tentacles, the clownfish protect their living home from such predators.

There are about ten species of anemones that are home to

136

137: The terminal-phase stoplight parrotfish used to be a
female but changed to be a male, with a completely different
coloration. (*Sparisoma viride*, Caribbean)
137: This initial-phase stoplight parrotfish is either a male or
a female, since both sexes, at their initial-phase, have the
same appearance. (*Sparisoma viride*, Caribbean)

137

anemonefishes and over 25 species of these fishes that cohabit with them. For some species of anemones, the protection offered by the clownfish is critical, as demonstrated when the fish are removed from the anemone by aquarium collectors. Having lost their protectors, these anemones are vulnerable to butterflyfish, which can nip off the anemone's tentacles (*84*). The tentacles are critical to the anemones' existence, because they are used to catch food, using nematocysts, and in some cases to make food, thanks to low densities of zooxanthellae that reside in the tentacles. Thus the removal of the anemonefish bodyguards may mean death for the anemone from tentacle-munching predators.

Clownfish are also good parents. The larger female clownfish lays eggs on the rock at the base of the anemone, but it becomes the male's duty to tend the nest during the week or so while the eggs develop. Depending on the species, the eggs change color from red with large yolks to the dark silvery color of the tiny embryonic fish with their reflective eyes. Males fan the nest, aerating the eggs and nipping here and there to remove damaged eggs.

Although this sounds wholesome enough, there is another side to the story. Mama used to be papa before she had a sex change. In anemonefishes, all young adults are male. When the female dies, the dominant male changes sex and produces eggs (*85*). Then one of the larger males, who is just hanging around waiting to become a real guy, becomes a functional male with the responsibility of fertilizing eggs and tending the nest. (Plates 138, 139)

Another nesting member of the damselfish family is the sergeant major. Males are good parents, but their territorial nature results in extra work (*86*). When the mating period arrives, which may depend on the season or phase of the moon, male sergeant majors select a patch of rock and clean it in order to prepare a nest. Females are enticed to the area and lay strings of eggs, which stick to the rock. The females are either chased away by the territorial male or just depart, leaving him with all the baby-sitting chores.

138: A parent orange-fin anemonefish guards its nest of red eggs protected under its home anemone (*Amphiprion chrysopterus*). (Fiji)
139a, b: As eggs develop, the eyes become visible as tiny, paired dark spots on each embryo (*Amphiprion chrysopterus*). (Fiji)

138

139a

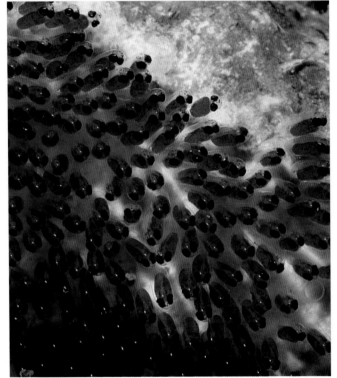

139b

140: The purple color of rocks behind these sergeant majors indicates a nest. (*Abudefduf saxatilis*, Caribbean)

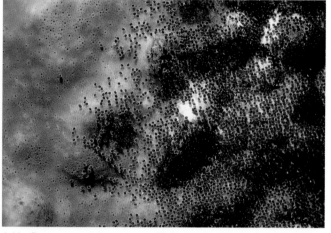

141: Sergeant major eggs will be protected by the male as they develop, over a period of a week or so, into embryos. Once the babies hatch, they will be on their own. (*Abudefduf saxatilis*, Caribbean)

From time to time, gangs of other fish descend on the nest and may overwhelm the poor male, who frantically dashes about nipping at the marauders. After the eggs hatch, the young receive no more baby-sitting services from papa. As with anemonefish, the eggs change color as the embryos develop—in this case from purple to a dark silver indicative of the yolk developing into tiny fish with shiny eyes. (Plates 140, 141)

From the liberated baby-sitting male damselfish we come to the chauvinistic, harem masters of Indo-Pacific reefs—basslets (*87*). These fish start out life as females whose appearance is relatively drab when compared to the more vividly colored males. The females are corralled, tended, and harassed by the male harem master. Male harassment affects the female endocrine system, keeping estrogen levels high and perpetuating femaleness. When a male disappears, though, the harassment ceases, hormone levels change, and the dominant female begins to act like a male. Within a couple of weeks she/he, has changed color, size, and shape to become a fully functional male, harassing the other females and keeping basslet society in order . . . at least according to the males. (Plate 142)

Getting Together

In human societies it isn't always easy to find the perfect mate . . . or even a compatible mate. Consequently, we have created all kinds of ways to get together. Singles discos (sometimes called "meet/meat-markets"), rock concerts, and other social events have the sometimes subtle, but ever-present, function of getting opposite sexes together for eventual reproduction. Marine animals also have their own rituals and events for insuring that eggs get fertilized. But many marine species have external fertilization where sperm and eggs are released to the environment with no parental involvement. In this case, selecting a mate for life is not as much an issue as insuring that eggs are fertilized and that young develop through their juvenile stages.

One solution is to have mass get-togethers. Like the basslets, some male bluehead wrasses spawn with groups of females, but their mating system is much more complicated than simply maintaining a harem. Most wrasses are like the parrotfish we mentioned earlier: They develop either as males or females, which look the same, but then some females change sex to become super-males or terminal-phase males. Even some of the initial-phase males can transform themselves to become super-males. These sex-changed,

142: These two colorful basslet males are harem masters, tending groups of the more drab females. Should a male die, one of the females will change sex and take over his duties. (*Pseudanthias squammipinnis*, Fiji)

143: A spawning aggregation of bluehead wrasse dart toward the surface where eggs and sperm will be released—away from many reef predators. (*Thalassoma bifasciatum*, Caribbean)

terminal-phase males are territorial; in contrast, neither the initial-phase males nor the females maintain territories (*88*). The females hang around reefs where currents bring in food for most of the day. Then, when it's time to spawn, they cruise down the reef to a spawning site. The site may be occupied by a terminal-phase male as a territory, or it may be so crowded with little males that it's a group spawn-site with no territoriality. Because there are more predators on the reef than in the open water above, the wrasses coordinate their spawning. At group spawn-sites, fish congregate in groups and then a female darts toward the surface, escorted by males, where, at the apex of their excursion, they simultaneously release sperm and eggs. At sites where territorial males dominate, spawning involves a male-female pair that darts toward the surface to spawn. The male has multiple spawnings but they are sequential each with a single female. This gets the fertilized eggs away from lurking predators below on the reef. Thus, a male gets a good return on his investment of maintaining a territory by having his sperm fertilize a number of the eggs. (Plates 143, 144)

144: The terminal-phase, male bluehead wrasse is easily differentiated from the yellow initial-phase that can be either male or female. (*Thalassoma bifasciatum*, Caribbean)

This is particularly advantageous for the territorial, terminal-phase males because they have the best chances of their sperm fertilizing eggs, but what about the other males? Some of them cheat! Hanging around a territory, these males act like females to avoid being chased away. When the territorial male and females spawn, the cheater "streaks" up and releases sperm as he passes (*89*). Sometimes a male just waits until the territorial male leaves for a moment and then "sneaks" in to spawn with an arriving female. Although the percentage of eggs fertilized by the territorial males is greater, these streakers and sneakers do get some eggs fertilized. For the species, the name of the game is making as many babies as possible. Thus, there are attempts to get around the territory holders' advantage: by overcoming him with numbers as the territories become group-spawning sites or by parasitizing him as sneakers and streakers take advantage of whatever opportunity arises.

Mass spawning has been taken to the extreme on the Great Barrier Reef where as many as 200 species of corals may spawn on the same night. Slicks of eggs and sperm coat the sea surface and extend for miles. In addition to insuring that eggs get fertilized, such synchronous spawnings may provide some degree of protection in numbers. Whatever predators might be ready to feed on the spawn are presumably quickly satiated by such an overwhelming amount of food. After consuming a tiny percentage of the total amount of spawn, what remains is left without further predation, at least for a while (*90*).

Diving in a snowstorm of sperm and eggs is certainly an experience but there is something even weirder. The most extraordinary sexual experience of my life occurred not in Thailand, the Philippines, or California but rather in the sea off Little Cayman Island, around 8 p.m. in August, when I descended to the reef and was immediately greeted by a sea cucumber, numbers of brittle stars, and some gorgonians all spawning. The gorgonians were particularly spectacular as they, like corals, were releasing a snow flurry of

145

gamete bundles (eggs and/or sperm) that swirled about the reef. I then noticed that my buddy was intently exploding passing worms by flicking them with his finger. Indignantly, I motioned him to stop killing these precious little creatures, but he directed me to look more closely. I then noticed these worms were only partial worms; they were missing their heads! The remainder of each worm remained safely in the reef to grow and reproduce again. These were palolo worms involved in their annual mass spawning. I had known of this phenomenon for years but had never been fortunate enough to witness it.

After photographing these worms, and with only a few shots left in my camera, I began my ascent. The drama increased the closer we approached the surface. Finally, I found myself engulfed in thousands of worms all exploding on their own and turning the water into a soup of sperm and eggs. Wow, what a mess! The visibility was terrible, but I did capture this "special moment" on the final frames in my camera. I sometimes wear a hood while diving at night, because I hate to have little crawly things swim into my ears,

146

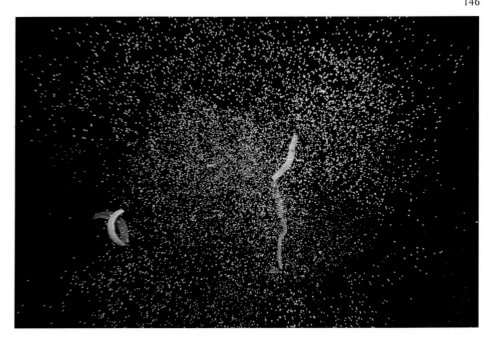

145, 146, and 147: Pink palolo worms engage in nocturnal, mass spawning events. Adults, living in reef crevices, release the posterior section of their bodies engorged with gametes that swim to the surface and "explode," releasing sperm and eggs. (*Eunice schemacephala*, Caribbean)

but this time it backfired on me. The sheer number of worms all wiggling in their sexual frenzy meant that some would make it into my hood and ultimately into my ears. Soon I too was involved in frantic agitation as the worms in my ears were driving me crazy. So this great event of sex in the sea ended with me flailing about, shaking my head and tearing at my hood, as I emerged from the water dripping with sperm and eggs ... and worms. (Plates 145, 146, 147)

147

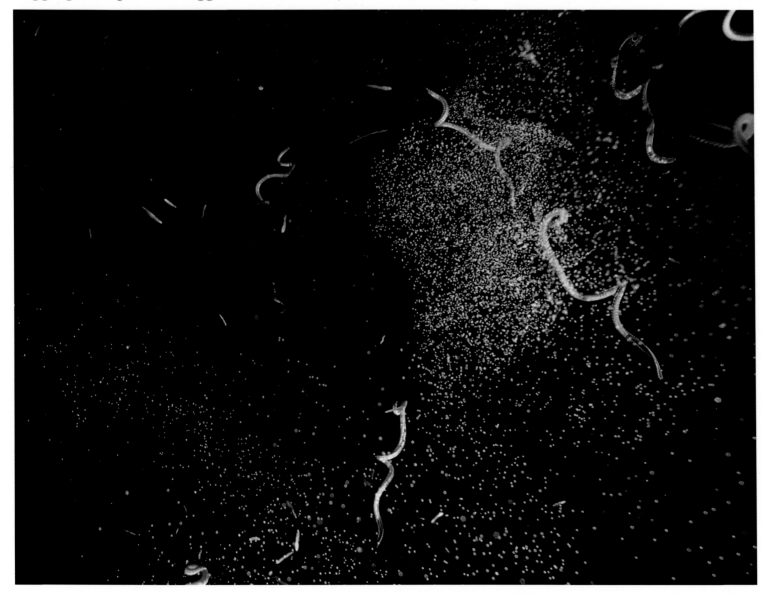

148: These nudibranchs face opposite directions and engage in reciprocal copulation. Each gives sperm to the other and both then depart as mothers to lay egg masses on the reef. (*Chromodoris lochi*, Fiji)

149: Asexual reproduction is common in some sea stars. A single arm of this sea star has detached and is now developing into a new individual. (*Linkia multifora*, Fiji)

From the far side of the sexual spectrum we have nudibranchs that are male and female at the same time. These beautiful snails without shells enjoy internal fertilization and, thus, must have the necessary anatomical equipment to make it happen. Consequently, their reproductive activities involve the supreme sexual experience of both giving and receiving. Of course, all of them also become mothers. Imagine what it would be like if humans developed such a strategy. It boggles the mind! (Plate 148)

Doing Without Sex

The good news about asexual reproduction is that it's easy. No problem finding a mate, no eggs to fertilize, and no risk in growing up. In budding or fragmentation, the individual gives rise to another individual. The "parent" has already proven itself successful by the fact that it is alive and able to reproduce. Thus, the survival chances for the "progeny" are very good. For corals this involves a division or extension of a polyp's tissue to form a sister polyp. In some sea stars, such as *Linkia* sp., an arm just detaches and crawls away. It's as though your biological clock started screaming and, tired of all of this male-female bother, you decided to do something really drastic. You pulled off an arm, set it on the mantle, and then sat back to enjoy the bliss of watching your child develop. No pregnancy, morning sickness, or strawberries and pickles. No little monster running around the house or bizarre teen-age misfit to rattle your cage—since the kid would be an exact replica of you. Depending upon the level of neurotic baggage you lug around, the experience could be quite nice or the worst nightmare imaginable. It might be something you should discuss with your roommate or partner first. (Plate 149)

There is No Best Strategy

Whether it be human cultures or reef species, there is incredible diversity in how individuals go about the important process of perpetuating their genes. Asexual reproduction is safe and relatively sure, but the down side is that there is no genetic mixing to facilitate adaptation and evolution. Sexual reproduction provides more variability as genes from parents are rearranged to create individuals different from each parent.

Another dimension of reproduction in the coral city is the energy invested in young. Some species like the bluehead wrasse may spawn every day of the year, releasing small eggs and sperm in huge amounts but which receive no protection or parental care. On the other hand, the clownfish and sergeant major create a nest, lay a small number of large eggs and actively protect them from intruders. Many sharks and rays, as well as mammals, provide the supreme protection, fertilizing eggs inside the female and then nurturing them until birth, but they produce very few young.

In order to provide a completely balanced discussion on the subject of sex, it needs to be said that there are many fish that "behave themselves," at least according to some human standards. There are species of butterflyfish and angelfish that are "good" fish; they pair, bond, and remain together for life. The biological advantage to this strategy is that they don't have to waste energy defending a territory against competitive males or worrying about such things as sneakers and streakers. (Plate 150)

150: Although many fish spawn indiscriminately with multiple partners over a lifetime, others like these fire gobies live together as mates. (*Nemateleotris magnifica*, Fiji)

CHAPTER EIGHT
Social Security

H AVING SPENT SOME TIME living with native peoples in places like Papua New Guinea and the Amazon, I have observed that those who have maintained the natural integrity of their local ecosystems have a remarkable degree of security. The forests and reefs not only supply them with a variety of foods but also with medicines and building materials such as wood, bamboo, and vines. I came to realize that these people, in a sense, were living in a grocery store, hardware store, and pharmacy, and as long as they did not become greedy the shelves would be restocked naturally. If the outside world of commerce ceased to exist, the quality of their lives would not appreciably change. And more importantly, they would not starve. It is unlikely we could ever hope for such social security in our "civilized" world.

Biodiversity

In the coral city, security depends on biological diversity. Within each species there are a variety of individuals, each with slightly different characteristics, capabilities, and tolerances. This variety is nature's way of dealing with unpredictable future change. When the sea level rises, or climate warms or cools, or diseases sweep through a population, or new competitors or predators arrive on the scene, individual variation or diversity insures that there will be at least a few individuals able to meet these challenges, to survive and to perpetuate the species. In addition to the genetic diversity within a species, the total variety of species is of the utmost importance to the security of the reef community (*91*). (Plate 151) Although the reef can tolerate the loss of a species, it is more vulnerable as its

151: Each species on the reef—whether it be a sponge, soft corals, algae, or a long-jaw squirrelfish (*Sargocentron* sp.)—has an ecological role, and the collective work of these reef residents creates a healthy community. (Palau)

135

152: As herbivores, sea urchins perform an important eco-logical role in controlling the growth of algae and keeping space available for other reef species. (*Diadema savignyi*, Fiji)

diversity is reduced. Removing a couple of rivets from an airplane may likewise have no observable effect, but with each lost rivet the plane becomes less secure, particularly under conditions of stress such as in a storm.

Actually, any good design accounts for a certain degree of unpredictability and builds in back-up systems or redundancy. Redundancy becomes extremely important when changes occur. In nature things change all the time. We know that such changes can be severe enough to cause the extinction of some species, but if there is ecological redundancy, where other species are performing the same function, the loss of one species may be compensated for by the other species. In other words, having an important ecological function performed by a number of different species offers ecological security and enables the ecosystem to persist even when a species is lost. Biological diversity is social security in the coral city.

Here's how it works. For example, as pointed out previously, the job of reef herbivores, such as urchins, parrotfish, and surgeonfish, is to mow the lawn of the reef and keep weeds from overgrowing. This is important because larval corals need open space for settlement. Since algae grow faster than corals, they can overgrow newly settled corals, depriving them of sunlight and access to zooplankton drifting in currents.

The lawnmowers offer ecological life insurance for the whole community. Reduction of parrotfish and surgeonfish populations by overfishing in the Caribbean has eliminated part of the community of lawnmowers, but sea urchins were generally able to take up the slack. Then in 1983, a disease swept through the Caribbean, virtually eliminating *Diadema* urchins as the reef's lawnmowers. In this case, ecological redundancy, which is really ecological social security, had already been lost due to overfishing of the fish lawnmowers. The loss of urchin lawnmowers resulted in an ecological disaster (*92*). Algae grew wildly, covering the bottom and creating difficult conditions for corals, both young and old. Problems for corals meant problems for the entire ecosystem. Fortunately, the genetic diversity of urchins, another form of security, lay in those few possessing immunity from the 1983 disease, and they are now repopulating the reefs, slowly. With the revival of urchins, the ecological balance may return in time, assuming reef management programs protect herbivorous fish from overfishing. (Plate 152)

Genetic diversity is easily demonstrated by the variety of colors we see in species, whether they be humans, worms, or crinoids. Of equal, if not greater importance, are the variations in a species' physiology and metabolism. Much of the variety in a species may be of no use or benefit at one particular moment in time, but as long as the differences do not reduce the survival of the individual, there will be no reason for them to be eliminated through evolution. In the future, though, some of those differences may be absolutely critical for an individual's survival. If, for example, environmental changes cause most individuals to die, then those with the proper variation in size, shape, color, or physiology may be the only ones to survive—the only ones to carry on the species. (Plates 153, 154, 155)

Many people who want to plan for their long-term security invest in mutual funds. The diversity of stocks in these funds insures a return even when some individual investments are not profitable or a company goes out of business. Imagine planning a community where the buildings are alive and produce food for its resi-

153, 154, and 155: Christmas tree worms decorate reefs in a rainbow of colors, visually demonstrating genetic diversity within the group. Such biodiversity is an important evolutionary investment, helping insure that at least a few individuals in generations to come will survive unpredictable environmental changes. (*Spirobranchus* sp., Caribbean and Fiji)

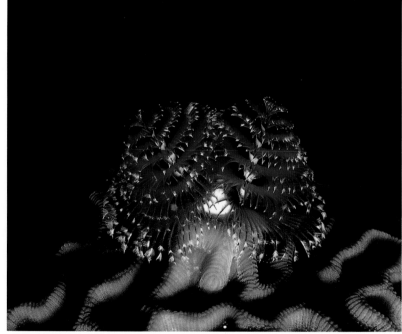

153

154

dents. Would it not be most prudent to design buildings of different tolerances, shapes, and other characteristics based on the understanding that only a few are likely to meet all the unpredictable challenges they face? In a sense this is just what the reef's planning department (the evolutionary process) has done over millions of years. Some corals do well in shallow water and others prefer deeper water where light is dim. Some tolerate heavy swells and others are

fragile. Some are good competitors for sunlight and space and others are not. Some are massive and grow slowly while others grow fast and in branches. The remarkable variety of forms, reproductive strategies, and ecological adaptations insure that after a crown-of-thorns infestation, typhoon, El Niño warming, or other unpredictable event, some species will survive to continue the important job of reef construction and food production. Unfortunately, the stresses we are inflicting on reefs are taking place so fast and in so many different forms that reefs as we know them are threatened (*93*). Nevertheless, some corals will assuredly survive, largely due to their different tolerances and preferred habitats. (Plate 156, 157)

156: Elkhorn corals dominate this shallow reef crest, growing fast and reaching toward the surface for sunlight and food, but many other species are involved, creating the reef as a whole. Other corals grow more slowly in massive or encrusting forms on deeper regions of the reef. Creating living buildings with a variety of tolerances and characteristics is the architectural wisdom of this city under the sea. (*Acropora palmata*, Caribbean)

Disturbance, Diversity, and Security

Change is an important aspect of ecology and community dynamics. After some form of disturbance, such as a typhoon or hurricane, diversity is reduced because many creatures have been wiped out. But with a reservoir of individuals nearby their progeny can recolonize the area and begin a process of community redevelopment. This is called succession and begins with a very few hardy

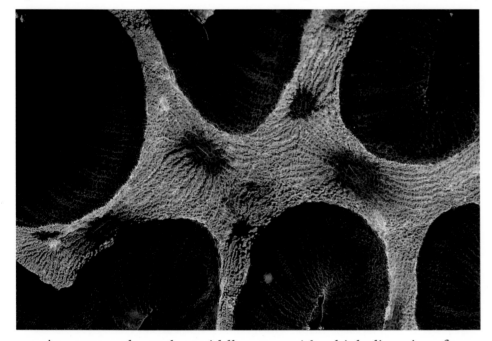

species, passes through a middle stage with a high diversity of species, and ends with fewer species as a result of better competitors eliminating some of the mid-phase species. This process has been documented on land after forest fires and in the sea after hurricanes, crown-of-thorns outbreaks, and other "catastrophes." It seems that a certain, intermediate level of disturbance is healthy for many ecosystems because it eliminates the dominants and provides opportunities for new species and new relationships between species to re-create viable communities (*94*). This means that coral reefs are not static ecosystems but are adapted to a certain degree of upheaval, which appears to have long-term benefits (*95*).

157: From the grand to the smallest of scales, corals display an incredible variety of architectural forms. This diversity reflects different adaptive strategies for survival under different conditions. We know that a diversity of coral species is good, and such variety and beauty is certainly a wonder of nature, but exactly how each fits into the reef's web of life remains a mystery to science. (Fiji)

158: A mushroom coral is not a colony. It is one single individual—the largest of all individual coral polyps. The brilliant pink and purple pigments are created by the animal rather than its algal partners. (*Fungia fungites*, Fiji)

But the intensity and frequency of the insults we are inflicting on reefs far exceeds this intermediate level of disturbance. The constant impact of nutrients and sediments, the continuation of excessive fishing, and the more frequent El Niños and warming events do not give the reefs time to restore themselves, and thus, like a forest burned too often, only the most hardy, weedy species can survive under such conditions. This means that reef species that require longer to settle and grow and that depend on other species, which also require more time and stable conditions, will be lost and diversity will decline. (Plates 158, 159, 160)

The human analogues are numerous. At the physical/structural level our cities with the most vitality are dynamic. Over the last 30 or more years any visit to New York or Hong Kong would have revealed perfectly functional buildings being torn down and replaced by ones more modern. The incredible costs of such revitalization have proven a good investment. At a more human level we have election years and revolutions. We know that bureaucracies and other institutions can get stagnant and unproductive. The solution to this problem is to rejuvenate the system. On the low disturbance side of the scale we call that rejuvenation and have an election where the old establishment is replaced with fresh ideas and personnel. On the high side of the disturbance scale we call the process a revolution. Too frequent elections hardly make a difference at all, as some in the United States claim, and if the disturbance is too infrequent, as with the dismantling of the Soviet Union in the 1990s, the change is so drastic that the entire system is threatened. Obviously, we have not yet found the optimum strategy for reducing stagnation and dominating institutions that stifle diversity in a meaningful and peaceful manner. But the reef at least offers some interesting ways of looking at dynamic processes that serve to revitalize communities and in some ways promote their long-term well-being.

159: Hundreds of tiny polyps create this staghorn coral colony (*Acropora* sp., Fiji). They share a common skeleton and because their digestive tracts are connected they share food as well.

160: As a reef regenerates after disturbance, diversity gradually increases until better competitors or longer-lived individuals reduce the number and variety of their neighbors. This biodiversity involves many species other than corals. Here a sailor's eyeball alga is surrounded by purple sea squirts, sponges, and other invertebrates. (*Ventricaria ventricosa*, Caribbean)

Innovation, Competition, Cooperation, and Selection

Western civilizations have chosen or fashioned what they feel offer good opportunities for social well-being and security. Ideally, capitalism contemplates a marketplace where people are free to create new goods or services, and others are free to select what best fits their needs. As producers compete for buyers in this marketplace, producers are perhaps "ideally" forced to improve their products to meet new challengers. Thus, those goods or services that are "inferior" in the eyes of the consumer, who is the selector (as in natural selection), disappear and those that have adapted better to meet the needs of the consumer survive. In this way, innovation creates products of higher quality and/or lowers their price, whether the products be detergents or computers, and then consumers select which ones will be more likely to survive in the marketplace.

We can take comfort in the fact that the principles of evolution, which are in many ways similar to capitalism, have been operating very well in nature for a few billion years. They have resulted in a diverse and remarkably sustainable planetary living system. Evolution is driven by variation, from mutations and the mixing of genetic factors or genetic recombination as in sexual reproduction, which is an important source of differences between individuals. Survival and reproductive success are determined by a variety of factors including competition, how well the individual meets environmental challenges, and how it interacts with individuals of other species, including cooperative relationships, as we have seen in previous chapters. The influence of these factors results in the survival of the fittest or more accurately the elimination of the less fit. So capitalism and evolution have a lot in common—variation, competition, cooperation, and selection. (Plate 161)

The issue of cooperation deserves a bit more attention since the focus of both evolution and capitalism has historically emphasized competition rather than cooperation. Competition requires energy, and we see many examples of organisms adjusting their habi-

161: Although these lizardfish may give the impression of a standoff, they are really cooperating. They wait until a school of silverside fish swim close, then they simultaneously attack. By working together they create greater confusion and have a better chance of catching a meal. (*Synodus* sp., Caribbean)

tats, food preference, and life styles to avoid the waste of conflict. We have seen that where many colonies of corals and soft corals meet there is an empty zone, a "no-man's-land" where both sides have retreated from battle. (Plate 162) In this way, niches (the various ways an organism uniquely adapts to the challenges of survival, from food to habitat to coloration to reproductive strategy) become narrower as ecosystem diversity increases, producing more special-

162: Orange soft corals (*Dendronephthya* sp.), yellow hard corals (Dendrophyllid coral), and other invertebrates turn a sunken warship, dedicated to killing, into a celebration of fertility and beauty. (Truk Lagoon)

ists and fewer generalists. An increase in specialization, whether it be a coral reef or a new business enterprise, is encouraged by competition. The incredible diversity and specialization of corals and reef fishes are examples. (Plate 163) In the human domain, the original, relatively simple automobiles and computers have each evolved into a remarkable diversity of specialized variants, autos,

163

and computers designed for very special uses rather than being limited to generalized all purpose models. Certainly, competition has been a driving force in innovation and diversity.

In a broader perspective, remaining competitive may require that cooperative alliances be forged. They are not mutually exclusive. Cooperation is obvious in the coral city where so many organisms depend on one another and have adapted to life in the coral city in so many strange ways. Corals and zooxanthellae mutually benefit each other, as do symbiotic cleaners and their hosts, as well as clownfish and anemones. (Plates 165-171) Some industries are now paying careful attention to the quality of life of their employees, by locating in attractive communities, offering child care, and providing fringe benefits to all employees rather than just executives. In fact, they are becoming involved in community programs to insure their employees remain in the area. They are remaining competitive through cooperative/mutualistic relations.

Lessons from the Reef

Can the coral city offer any guidance for those of us hoping to improve our own communities? Certainly coral cities are better organized than most human communities in terms of population control, efficient use of limited resources, productivity, food and energy security, waste and pollution reduction, recycling, community integration, and back-up systems that promote the long-term survival of the community. In spite of present economic dogma, our planet does not have unlimited resources. Thus, maintaining any semblance of quality of life for the future requires that we must deal with these critical issues, many of which have already been resolved in the coral city, particularly overpopulation, over-consumption of natural resources, and environmental degradation.

What would life be like in a city based on the model of a coral reef? First of all, it would be a place full of living things. All streets, sidewalks, and open spaces would be decorated with plants,

164

163: The reef is a dynamic ecosystem in constant change; yet, through innovation, competition, cooperation, and natural selection there is a sufficient stability to achieve sustainability. Here, orange soldierfish (*Myripristis* sp.) and a golden damselfish (*Amblyglyphidon aureus*) seek refuge beneath giant sea fans. (Fiji)

164: Some massive coral heads, like this star coral, may be a few hundred years old, as indicated by internal growth rings such as those on a tree. Chemical analysis of old coral skeletons can provide information about past climate, showing both temperature and rainfall. (*Montrastrea annularis*, Caribbean)

165: Whether by genetic abberation, disease, or parasite, genes that create the typical labyrinthine form of a brain coral have changed their message and directed the creation of a completely different form in the center of this image. (*Leptoria phrygia*, Fiji)

166: A purple sponge (*Nara nematifera*) invades a coral (Favid coral) in the constant struggle for food and space. (Palau)

167: In a world of solar collectors, pink coralline algae grow over this green and brown coral, which derives its color from the zooxanthellae (algae) living inside it. (*Blastomussa merleti*, Fiji)

168: An entire ecosystem in miniature: We see a green coral that is both producer and consumer and a red sponge that is consumer and recycler. Waste products of the reef may be digested and released as nutrients by the sponge. The nutrients may be utilized by algae living in the coral to make food used by the coral to make mucus that may be taken up by the sponge to complete the cycle. (Caribbean)

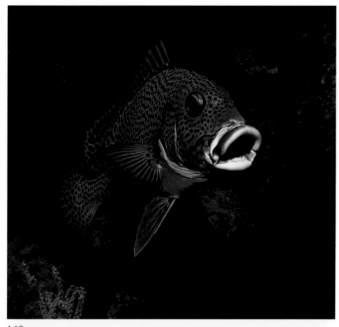

169

170

169 and 170: Variations on a theme of mouth. Expanded lips of the aptly named spotted sweetlips (*Plectorhinchus picus*) presumably help it detect and suck in a meal, while the scribbled filefish mouth (*Aluterus scriptus*) is more adapted for nipping. (Fiji)

but the natural decor would actually be edible and functional, as the plants would be producing fruits, vegetables, and useful materials such as wood, fibers, and medicines. In addition to products, trees and other vegetation provide other important functions such as taking up CO_2 and air pollutants, producing oxygen, and providing air conditioning through shade. In some areas community gardens would be maintained and protected by local residents. The buildings would be roofed with solar panels to provide energy and hot water for the community. All waste from the building's kitchens and toilets would be used to fertilize roof-top gardens or the edible landscaping. Lest all of those plants get out of hand, herbivores would act as natural lawnmowers controlling growth and converting plant production into animal resources of meat, fur, leather, milk, eggs, and so on.

There would be a great variety of architectural designs to provide space for a greater variety of uses, including nurseries and apartments, some of which would be shared by both day workers and night workers. In addition, air conditioning, waste treatment, and recycling would take place inside these buildings or adjacent to them. In fact, there would be no waste, because byproducts of one activity or product would become raw materials for another. Debris such as old bricks and cement from inner city revitalization would be reused in future construction. Raw materials imported from outside would be efficiently used and carefully managed. It would be a colorful city of modest size since it would need considerable open space dedicated to collecting solar energy and producing food on site. There would be relatively few imports or exports since the city would be mostly self-sufficient.

A rich variety of cultures and life-styles would exist. Residents would still dress up, socialize to find mates, and engage in a variety of personal lifestyles. Individual or community-based systems for population control would be in effect. Public health services would be available and a wide variety of cooperatives and working associations would exist. There would still be some false advertising and thieves. Conflict would not disappear, but it would not escalate into self-destructive warfare as we have seen in the human domain. We would continue to enlist other species such as dogs for personal protection and companionship. We would also open our communities to a variety of other non-human visitors such as song birds, butterflies, and bees, since the work they do in pollinating our edible and functional landscapes would be highly valued. Obviously, our means of controlling pests would not include toxic chemicals that could undermine the free services provided by such pollinators.

And this city would not be silent either. Just as shrimp snap to ward off intruders or stun a meal, as parrotfish scrape and grind up coral, or as some fish such as the toadfish and some damselfish make noises to attract a mate and thus to communicate with each other, so would our city retain the sounds of productivity and communication.

Business would be based mostly on the capitalist model with a diversity of products and services available. Instead of a growth economy, there would be a dynamic equilibrium wherein some businesses would fail while others would be growing and thriving, depending on competition and changing consumer needs. This dynamism and diversity would avoid stagnation and insure that basic community needs would be met even during recessions. There would also be a place for socialism, but these sub-communities and co-ops would need to compete as effective members of the greater community. Individual portfolios and mutual funds would still benefit from a diversity of investment strategies.

Regular elections would eliminate obsolete bureaucracies and revitalize the community, just as typhoons and forest fires are important for the long-term health and vitality of some ecosystems.

At all levels considerable investment would be made in research and development, creating a diverse knowledge base that would be reflected in a variety of future goods and services. Specifically, in such a community the value of basic research would not be questioned—the benefits would be obvious. While petroleum reserves are abundant we would invest heavily in energy sources not based on petroleum, in preparation for the days when the reserves are gone. Certainly, a major focus would be renewable energy, such as photovoltaic, wind, biomass, waves, tides, and the like. Such investments would ensure that the community could adapt and meet unpredictable challenges from outside the immediate region of the community.

Finally, perhaps the most important lesson to be learned from nature is that cooperation is essential in achieving sustainability. One very pragmatic reason is the realization of the interconnectedness of all species and even species and the environment—the premise that everything is connected. Any species, including *Homo sapiens*, that undermines the ecological integrity of the ecosystem undermines the security of its own future. In the human domain, pollution and over-exploitation of resources obviously undermine the quality of life for everyone, including generations to come. Whether it be at the invertebrate level on coral reefs, in the sophisticated social systems in dolphin societies, or in our major cities, all organisms are mutually dependent on one another through the roles they play in maintaining ecological integrity.

Everything is Connected

We should not let our fascination with individual members of the coral community and the details of their personal stories prevent us from an appreciation of the whole. An important message of this book is that everything is connected, and, as such, everything has a value in promoting the fantastic complexity that keeps the entire community functioning. This is relevant to coral reefs, human communities, and the planet. It means that our influence on the planet, particularly in the domain of habitat, biological species, and genetic diversity, is undermining the habitability of the planet for ourselves. Three and one-half billion years of evolutionary experimentation and design for survival have created a living system more wonderful, creative, beautiful, and inspirational than any human could have ever imagined. Whether one considers a rainforest or a coral reef or the entire planet, these living communities defy the "laws of entropy," running, adapting, and restoring themselves all by themselves, taking random units of non-living raw materials and converting them into magnificent living things. What a treasure to be cherished and protected.

My hope in exploring these great structures and fascinating ecosystems, the coral cities, is to convey some knowledge that will help us feel more connected to the reef and all other living creatures on this life-supporting oasis in space. It might even encourage some of us to help redesign our communities and the ways we live. Whether it be a human community, the coral reef, or the planet, biological diversity is social security. Protecting it is protecting ourselves.

171: A feather star slowly crawls to the top of the reef at dusk to unfurl its arms and await the emergence of reef plankton. (*Lapromitra sp.*, Fiji)

172: Powered by the sun, a reef community passes through the natural stages of life, death, and eventual rejuvenation. A star coral colony (*Montastrea cavernosa*) is invaded and excavated by red sponges (*Cliona delitrix*) and a feather-duster worm (*Sabellastarte magnifica*). (Caribbean)

algae: An imprecise term applying to simple phototrophic organisms lacking complex reproductive structures. This group includes cyanophytes (blue-green algae, which are protists lacking a nuclear membrane), chrysophytes (diatoms), pyrrhophytes (dinoflagellates, which include zooxanthellae), chlorophytes (green algae), phaeophytes (brown algae), and rhodophytes (red algae). Most algae are aquatic. These organisms serve as solar collectors on the reef. Some are fleshy and plant-like, while others are thin encrustations growing over coral, such as the crustose coralline red algae. Zooxanthellae live inside corals and produce food that is used by the coral animal.

AMA: American Medical Association.

amino acid: The fundamental structural unit of proteins. There are only twenty or so amino acids, containing carbon, hydrogen, nitrogen, and oxygen atoms, and all have the same basic structure. The way in which amino acids are arranged in different proteins determines their various properties.

Anthozoa: A class of the phylum Cnidaria that includes sea anemones, sea fans, and stony corals.

anthropogenic: Arising from human activities.

asexual reproduction: The reproduction of a new individual without involvement of a mate or fertilization, as in the union of two gametes. In corals, this is accomplished either by fragmentation or budding. *See also* **fragmentation**

atoll: A ring-shaped, flat coral reef surrounding a lagoon, which is perched on top of a foundation, such as a volcano, that over time may have gradually sunk or subsided, leaving the ring of coral reef behind.

base pairs: A pair of nitrogenous bases (one purine, which is either adenine or guanine; the other pyrimidine: either cytosine or thymine) that connect the two strands of the double helix that comprises the two complimentary deoxyribonucleic acids in terms of their nucleotide bases: A and T or C and G. Base pairing is also present in RNA (ribonucleic acid). *See* **DNA**

biodiversity, biological diversity: Refers to variations or diversity of physiology, anatomy, or behavior within a species, or a variety of species in a community, or a variety of habitats and communities on land or in the sea. Biodiversity has proven to be important for the survival of species and communities. Presently, the world is experiencing an alarming period of declining diversity due to human activities.

bio-eroders: Organisms, such as snails, sponges, and parrotfish, that slowly excavate bits of reef. *See also* **intertidal notch**

"biological desert": The open sea where nutrients are in short supply.

biosystems: Living organisms that perform work as does a machine.

black-band disease: A community of organisms, of which blue-green algae (Cyanobacteria) is dominant, that digest coral tissue. The organisms collectively appear dark and advance across coral as a black band, leaving a white coral skeleton behind. *See also* **white-band disease**

bleaching: A phenomenon where the zooxanthellae residing inside coral tissue are lost, causing the coral to appear white due to the transparent tissue and white skeleton below. Bleaching can be a natural process or can be caused by stress to corals from elevated water temperature and other factors. If corals remain bleached for too long they will die.

"blooms": A rapid increase in the number of individuals in a population. An example is the outbreaks or population "explosions" of dinoflagellates that result in fish kills and other ecological disruptions. Some shellfish filter dinoflagellates from the water and retain the toxins, which makes the shellfish poisonous to eat. *See also* **dinoflagellates**

blue-green algae: A cyanophyte, a primitive group of algae that lack a nuclear membrane (prokaryote) and are considered a form of bacteria. Some of these algae are capable of fixing nitrogen.

calcium carbonate: $CaCO_3$. It is the basic substance of the coral skeleton secreted by the coral polyp. As the reef grows from the buildup of coral skeletons, the calcium carbonate becomes compacted into a rock, limestone, which often accumulates over a course of millions of years to create massive geological structures.

character displacement: A change in an individual organism's characteristics in order to distinguish more easily one species from another species.

chlorophyll: The green pigment that absorbs light and converts it into chemical energy. This pigment is essential in the process of photosynthesis whereby algae and plants make food. *See also* **photosynthesis**

commensalism: The relationship involving two species that live together, whereby one organism benefits another while the other is neither harmed nor helped. *See also* **symbiosis**

conotoxins: A suite of peptide compounds used by cone snails to paralyze their prey. Such chemicals are proving useful in medicine to alleviate pain.

coral, corals: The individual coral animal is a coral polyp. The polyp secretes around itself a cup of hard calcium carbonate, which is the coral skeleton. The polyp and the skeleton are called coral. There are more than 700 different species of corals, all belonging to the Order Scleractinian (Phylum Cnidaria), that are the primary modern reef-building corals. See also **coral animal**

coral-algal relationship: A symbiotic relationship whereby the coral offers habitat, protection, and raw materials to algae-zooxanthellae. The algae in turn use the raw materials to produce food (carbohydrates) through photosynthesis. This food is then made available to the coral and becomes an important source of its nutrition. The algae also facilitate the coral's ability to create its skeleton.

coral animal: A synonym for coral polyp. *See* **coral, corals**

coralline algae: Red algae of the phylum Rhodophyta. Some are erect and branching while others are encrusting, like cement. The encrusting coralline algae serve as mortar that binds reef fragments together and solidifies the reef into one durable structure. These algae cover most surfaces of the reef, even where there is no coral. They often appear as a pinkish veneer over the surfaces, in some cases like a layer of cement.

coral bleaching: *See* **bleaching**

corallite: The external skeletal structure of an individual coral polyp composed of calcium carbonate. For colonial corals, many corallites make up the larger skeleton, called a corallum.

demersal zooplankton: Animal plankton that emerge at night. The derivative of the word is as follows: drifting (planktos) animals (zoo) that live in association with the bottom (demersal).

dinoflagellates: A member of the phylum Pyrrhophyta that is also considered a class of Protozoa. Generally, these organisms possess two flagella. Many dinoflagellates are able to ingest food from outside, as do animals, and at the same time synthesize their own food through photosynthesis. Some members are extremely toxic and cause fish kills, paralytic shellfish poisoning, and amnesic poisoning. Zooxanthellae are dinoflagellates.

DMZ: Demilitarized zone, i.e., a no-man's-land.

DNA: Deoxyribonucleic acid is the compound in which our genetic information is stored. It is the macromolecule found in a chromosome that specifies protein production by way of RNA. DNA consists of two complementary chains of polynucleotides wound into a double helix.

echinoderms: Spiny-skinned animals of the phylum Echinodermata that includes sea stars (starfish), brittle stars, feather stars, sea urchins, and sea cucumbers. The derivative of the word is "echino" (spine), plus "derm" (skin).

ecosystem, ecosystems: A functional unit of organisms (plants, animals, and microbes) along with the physical and chemical factors that affect the organisms and are in turn affected by them. This includes the biotic (species) and abiotic factors (physical and chemical aspects such as rainfall, salinity, temperature, and the like).

El Niño: An oceanographic and atmospheric phenomenon in the tropical Pacific Ocean, also called the El Niño Southern Oscillation (ENSO), in which the waters become unusually warm. During an El Niño, sea surface temperatures rise, westward trade winds diminish, and rainfall patterns change dramatically. Normally, trade winds cause the sea level to be one-half meter higher in the western Pacific around Indonesia and Australia. Due to the warmer waters, which extend deeper off the coasts of Ecuador and Peru, upwelling does not bring cold nutrient rich water to the surface. Without this fertilizer, phytoplankton productivity declines, resulting in a diminished abundance of food for the entire food chain. Fish move elsewhere or die, as do sea birds. Effects of these ocean/atmospheric conditions ripple around the planet affecting weather in other oceans and on all continents. Some regions experience abnormally heavy rainfall; in other regions, dry conditions prevail. The El Niño of 1997–98 had a serious impact on coral reefs, where warm waters caused corals to bleach and die in many oceans. La Niña is another oceanographic/atmospheric phenomenon, where ocean and weather conditions are opposite to those of El Niño. *See also* **La Niña**

entropy: A measure of the degree of disorder in a system. Maximum entropy means maximum disorder. Biology and nature work against entropy, and from disorder they create very orderly and organized species and ecosystems; but living systems must do work to keep themselves orderly, otherwise they will increase in entropy and thus increase in disorder.

evolution: In a Darwinian sense, evolution is the process whereby changes occur in species over a period of time that can lead to different lineages and to the origin of new species. Evolution takes place mainly through a process of variation (i.e., now understood to occur through recombination of genes and through mutations) and natural selection (i.e., nonrandom elimination of individuals), which results in, and is an important source of, differences among individuals. Selection and reproductive success between individuals or populations can be attributed to a variety of factors including competition, mutualism, and environmental challenges, resulting in individuals better adapted or designed for survival. Since the evidence supporting Darwin's theory (1859) has been overwhelming and so far not refuted by any alternative explanation, evolution in a Darwinian sense is considered by most scientists to be the defining paradigm and the unifying framework of biology.

foraminifera: A class of one-celled animals (Protozoans) some of which live as plankton, while others live on the ocean floor (benthic). Skeletons of foraminifera that have become compressed as sedimentary rock are now used as chalk for blackboards; they were also the building blocks of the pyramids.

fragmentation: A form of asexual reproduction. Pieces of coral broken off from the reef by wave action or storm surges may retain living tissue and eventually re-establish themselves as viable colonies.

gamete bundles: Packets of either sperm or eggs released by corals during spawning.

gene, genes: A unit or substance of heredity that determines a particular characteristic of an organism. It was once thought to be a particular place (locus) on a chromosome that determined a characteristic, but now it has been found that one characteristic may be affected by a number of genes or one gene may affect a number of different characteristics.

genome: The genome of any living organism is the genetic information contained in its DNA. It can be understood by regarding the genome as a book that contains all the information about how to construct that organism. The information is contained in the characters of text expressed as letters (A, T, C, G) in the genetic material. *See also* **human genome**

global warming: Atmospheric warming that heats the atmosphere and oceans, causing climate change that in some cases causes corals to bleach and die worldwide. *See also* **greenhouse effect**

greenhouse effect, greenhouse gases: The process whereby gasses in the atmosphere allow short wavelength light from the sun to pass through but retain longer wavelength light (heat). The result of this is that not all of the energy coming to the earth is able to return to space and thus the atmosphere is warmed. Since the age of industrialization, people have been releasing greenhouse gasses, such as carbon dioxide from the burning of fossil fuels, causing a rise in the temperature of the earth. This is one source of climate change that may have dire consequences for humans and for many natural ecosystems.

herbivores: Creatures that eat plants, such as algae and seagrasses, on the reef—e.g., the "lawnmowers," such as sea urchins, parrotfish, and surgeonfish. A reduction in the number of herbivores can give rise to a wide range of ecological consequences from an overgrowth of algae, many of which are quite serious.

human genome: The human genome is the full complement of our genetic blueprint or genetic information. This information is contained in the arrangement of four bases—A (adenine), T (thymine), G (guanine), and C (cytosine)—on a strand of DNA. The human genome, containing between 30,000 and 40,000 genes, is composed of more than three billion of these letters. The nucleus of every ordinary cell in the human body contains two chromosomes, each of which contains an entire genome.

human genome project: The human genome project is the scientific effort to decode the genome's blueprint (letters in the four-letter alphabet) sequentially, that is to say, in the correct order.

Hydrozoa: A class of the phylum Cnidaria that includes stony fire corals, hydroids, and the Portuguese Man-O-War.

"inducible defenses": Protective chemicals produced by some algae, sponges, and corals, which can be turned on after a predator grazes on them.

initial-phase males: Male wrasses and parrotfish that begin life as a male and stay that way. Some females may change sex and become "super-males" having an entirely different appearance from either males or females of the same species.

intertidal notch: Excavations of limestone shoreline by bio-eroders such as algae, chitons, snails, and sea urchins. These organisms contribute to re-modeling of the shoreline. *See also* **bio-eroders**

"junk DNA": Non-coding regions of DNA that appear not to be functioning as genes. They may once have played a role in evolution, or may play a role in future evolution, or may have other, hitherto unknown functions. *See* **DNA**

junk food: A term that refers to food produced by zooxanthellae and used by corals. Junk food is poor in nitrogen.

La Niña: An oceanographic/atmospheric phenomenon in the tropical Pacific Ocean where sea surface temperatures become cooler and rainfall and drought patterns are opposite to those of the El Niño condition. *See also* **El Niño**

"laws of entropy." *See* **entropy**

limestone: A form of calcareous, sedimentary rock. The major components of much limestone are coral skeletons that have become compacted through time and geological processes.

morphology: The study of changes in form. In the case of corals, wave action or other outside forces will change the form and shape of the coral.

mutualism: A relationship whereby both partners benefit. A category of symbiosis. *See also* **symbiosis**

nematocysts: Tiny capsules containing harpoon-like threads that, when activated, shoot out, impaling the victim, and often injecting venom into the victim. Nematocysts on the tentacles of anemones sting and catch food. They are also used for defense, as we learn when stung by a jellyfish.

neurotoxins: Chemical compounds that disrupt normal nerve function. Many marine organisms use such chemicals to deter predators or paralyze prey.

"niches": The unique way a species earns a living, survives, and reproduces in an ecosystem. According to ecological theory, each species occupies a unique niche.

nutrients: Substances that are necessary for sustaining life. Many substances such as nitrogen, phosphorus, and iron are important and in limited supply. Coral reef communities are adapted to low nutrient concentrations, and, if nutrients increase, ecological imbalances may occur.

ocelli, ocellus: Lens-like structures in giant clams that allow light to penetrate into the mantle tissue where zooxanthellae thrive.

opioids: Compounds that mimic or act similarly to the opium family of compounds.

ostracoderms: These were the first fish in fossil history. Protected by armored scales, and lacking jaws, they lived 450 million years ago and gave rise to sharks and the more advanced bony fishes.

parasites, parasitism: A relationship whereby one species benefits at the expense of the other. A category of symbiosis. *See also* **symbiosis**

pedicellariae: Small pincers on the surface of some echinoderms. These pincers serve as seizing organs to protect the organism from predators and from small creatures that might settle on the surface of the echinoderm. Urchins may have venomous or non-venomous pedicellariae.

Permian extinction: The period at the end of the Paleozoic era (220–270 million years ago), when the earth experienced the greatest loss of species, both on land and in the sea, probably from some cataclysmic event. After this, reptiles that were already flourishing gave rise to the dinosaurs.

photosynthesis: The process by which the solar energy of sunlight, with the aid of chlorophyll, is converted into the chemical energy of food. This involves carbon dioxide and water being converted into sugar (glucose) with the release of oxygen as a byproduct.

phytoplankton: The generally microscopic algae that drift as plankton. These include diatoms, dinoflagellates, and blue-green algae. *See also* **plankton**

plankton: Organisms that do not have control over their movements and drift with the currents. They may be algae (phytoplankton) or animals (zooplankton).

planulae: The tiny larvae of coral polyps, which swim freely and then settle to become a new coral. They search for hard surfaces on which to settle, often carried by currents to distant reefs.

polyp: An individual animal of the phylum Cnidaria (class Anthozoa or Hydrozoa). A polyp has tentacles with nematocysts that are used to catch prey or for defense.

primary productivity: The conversion of solar energy into chemical energy (bound in the chemical bonds of carbohydrates) by plants through the process of photosynthesis. This is the primary source of food that supports animals. *See also* **photosynthesis**

protein: Proteins are universally present and involved in everything that happens in a living organism. Some proteins are structural, such as connective tissue; others are involved in chemical reactions as enzymes. Protein is comprised of amino acids. Proteins fold themselves into various shapes, which designate their functions.

radula: A rough, tongue-like organ covered with sharp teeth found in snails, chitons, and some octopuses. It is used to scrape algae from the bottom or drill holes in the shells of prey organisms.

rudist bivalves: One of the two largest groups of giant clams that have ever existed on planet Earth. They became extinct around 70 million years ago.

rugose corals: Most probably the ancestors of modern Scleractinian corals. Their skeletal forms grew sequentially, rather than cyclically.

Scleractinian corals: Hard corals of the class Anthozoa. They are the most important modern reef builders, but relatively late arrivals in the fossil record (originating about 237 million years ago).

Scyphozoa: A class of the phylum Cnidaria that includes all the jellyfishes.

secondary metabolites: Chemical byproducts that, through metabolic processes, have become useful; for example, sponges produce certain metabolic waste products that are further changed into toxic materials that defend the sponge from predation.

septa: In coral, skeletal elements radiating inward toward the center from the corallite. *See also* **corallite**

setae: Bristles or hair-like structures on polychaete worms, which can be very irritating to skin.

"shut-down reaction": Rapid death of coral due to a spontaneous disintegration of coral tissue, probably due to any of a number of stresses or even a diver's fin-kick.

stromatolites: A pillar-shaped structure created by blue-green algae (cyanophytes). These structures have been around for over one billion years and still exist as living communities in the Bahamas and in Australia.

succession: A process whereby suites of species colonize and sequentially occupy a section of reef or landscape, beginning with a few hardy individuals that are generalists, passing through a middle stage with a high diversity of species, and ending with fewer species that may be specialists and better competitors.

super-male: Sex-changed individuals of a species of parrotfish or wrasse. Super-males began life as females and then changed to become males. The change into a "super-male" is prompted by a species adjustment in male-to-female ratios. *See also* **terminal-phase males; initial-phase males**.

sustainable, sustainability: Derived from the word "sustain," this word means to keep in existence, to maintain, to supply with necessities, to endure, and to withstand. In the context of human communities this means that they are managed in such a way as to maintain themselves through time without running out of raw materials and without creating harmful byproducts such as pollution, which disrupts vital processes and undermines a community's ability to continue. For instance, using solar energy is more sustainable than using fossil fuel because petroleum will eventually run out and because its use causes pollution. Likewise, reusing waste as a resource is more sustainable than throwing it away and causing pollution.

symbiosis: A relationship whereby individuals of two species living together interact in some way.

terminal-phase males: Another name for the sex-changed, super-males that look completely different from females or initial-phase males. *See also* **super-male; initial-phase males**

tetrodotoxin: A potent poison found in the pufferfish family. It is a neurotoxin produced by bacteria in the puffer's gut.

white-band disease: An unknown pathogen or factor that results in coral-tissue death, exposing a white skeleton. *See also* **black-band disease**

zooxanthellae: Unicellular algae that live inside coral tissue. They belong to the order of dinoflagellates in the phylum Pyrrophyta (and/or Protista). Zooxanthellae are essential to the survival of corals because they provide the corals with food and rid corals of waste. Corals may die when deprived of their zooxanthellae.

REFERENCES

1. Ehrlich, P. R. et. al. 1977. *EcoScience: Population, Resources, Environment*. W. H. Freeman and Co., New York.

   Duxbury, A. B., and A. C. Duxbury. 1996. *Fundamentals of Oceanography*. Wm. C. Brown Publishers, Dubuque, Iowa.

   Purves, W. K. et al. 2001. *Life: The Science of Biology*. W. H. Freeman and Co., New York.

2. Muscatine. L. 1990. "The Role of Symbiotic Algae in Carbon and Energy Flux in Reef Corals." In: Z. Dubinsky, ed. *Ecosystems of the World*, vol. 25: Coral Reefs.

3. Muscatine, L., and J. Porter. 1977. "Reef Corals: Mutualistic symbioses adapted to nutrient-poor environments." *BioScience* 27(7):454–460.

4. McCloskey, L. R.., and L. Muscatine. 1984. "Production and respiration in the Red Sea coral, *Stylophora pistillata*, as a function of depth." *Proceedings of the Royal Society of London*, Series B 222:215–30.

5. Klumpp, D. W., and J. S. Lucas. 1994. "Nutritional ecology of the giant clams *Tridacna tevoroa* and *T. derasa* from Tonga; influence of light on filter-feeding and photosynthesis." *Marine Ecology Progress Series* 107:147–156.

   Yonge, C. M. 1975. "Giant Clams." *Scientific American* 232 (4):96–105.

6. Dove, S. G. et al. 2001. "Major colour patterns of reef-building corals are due to a family of GFP-like proteins." *Coral Reefs* 19:197–204.

   Salih, A. et al. 2000. "Fluorescent pigments in corals are photoprotective." *Nature* 408(6814):850–853.

7. McCloskey, L. R. et al. 1994. "Daily photosynthesis, respiration, and carbon budgets in a tropical marine jellyfish (*Mastigias* sp.)." *Marine Biology* 119:13–22.

8. Hixon, M. A., and W. N. Brostoff. 1996. "Succession and herbivory: effects of differential fish grazing on Hawaiian coral-reef algae." *Ecological Monographs* 66:67–90.

9. Hillis-Colinvaux, L. 1986. "Historical perspectives on algae and reefs: have reefs been misnamed?" *Oceanus* 29 (2):43–48.

10. Brugemann, J. H. et al. 1996. "Bioerosion and sediment ingestion by the Caribbean parrotfish *Scarus vetula* and *Sparisoma viride*: implications of fish size, feeding mode and habitat use." *Marine Ecology Progress Series* 134:59–71.

    Horn, M. H. 1989. "Biology of marine herbivorous fishes." *Oceanography and Marine Biology* 27:167–272.

11. Payrot-Clausade, M. et al. 2000. "Sea Urchin and fish bioerosion on La Reunion and Moorea Reefs." *Bulletin of Marine Science* 66(2):477–485.

12. Hackney, J. M., Carpenter, R. C., and W. H. Adey. 1989. "Characteristic adaptations to grazing among algal turfs on a Caribbean coral reef." *Phycologia* 28:109–119.

    Hatcher, B. G., and A. W. D. Larkum. 1983. "An experimental analysis of factors controlling the standing crop of the epilithic algal community on a coral reef." *Journal of Experimental Marine Biology and Ecology* 69:61–84.

13. Ehrlich, P. R. et al. 1977. *EcoScience: Population, Resources, Environment*.

    Purves, W. K. et. al. 2001. *Life: The Science of Biology*.

14. Bruggemann, J. H. et al. 1996. "Bioerosion and sediment ingestion."

    Frydl, P., and C. W. Stearn. 1978. "Rate of bioerosion by parrotfish in Barbados reef environments." *Journal of Sedimentary Petrology* 48(4):1149–1158.

    Payrot-Clausade, M., et al. 2000. "Sea Urchin and fish bioerosion."

15. Bakus, G. J. 1973. "The biology and ecology of tropical holothurians." In: Jones, O. A., and R. Endean, eds. *Biology and Geology of Coral Reefs*, II. Academic Press, New York.

16. Todd, N. J., and J. Todd. 1984. *Bioshelters, Ocean Arks, City Farming: Ecology as the Basis of Design*. Sierra Club Books, San Francisco.

    Uhl, C., and A. Anderson. 2001. "Green Destiny: Universities Leading the Way to a Sustainable Future." *BioScience* 51(1):36–42.

17. Wilkinson, C. R. 1978. "Microbial associations in sponges. I. Ecology and physiology and microbial populations of coral reefs sponges." *Marine Biology* 49:161–167.

18. Reiswig, H. M. 1974. "Water transport, respiration and energetics of three tropical marine sponges." *Journal of Experimental Marine Biology and Ecology* 14:231–249.

19. Hallock, P. 1997. Reefs and Reef Limestones in Earth History. In: C. Birkeland, ed. *Life and Death of Coral Reefs*. University of Guam. Chapman and Hall.

20. Ladd, H., and S. Schlanger. 1960. "Drilling Operations on Eniwetok Atoll." U. S. Geological Survey, Professional papers, 260-Y. U. S. Government Printing Office, Washington, D.C.

21. Kuhlmann, D. H. H. 1985. *Living Coral Reefs of the World*. Arco Publishing, New York.

22. Loya, Y. 2000. "Homage to *Stylophora pistillata*: An important coral in core reef research." Abstract. 9th International Coral Reef Symposium. Bali, Indonesia.

23. Hixon, Mark. 1991. "Predation and Community Structure." In: P. Sale, ed. *The Ecology of Fishes on Coral Reefs*. Academic Press, New York.

    Hobson, Edmund S. 1991. "Trophic Relationships of Fishes Specialized to Feed on Zooplankters above Coral Reefs." In: P. Sale, ed. *The Ecology of Fishes on Coral Reefs*. Academic Press, New York.

    Luckhurst, B. E., and K. Luckhurst, 1978. "Diurnal space utilization in coral reef fish communities." *Marine Biology* 49:317-323.

24. Pearse, A. S. 1932. "Inhabitants of certain sponges at Dry Tortugas." Carnegie Institute of Washington Papers, Tortugas Laboratory 28:117–124.

25. Westinga, E., and P. C. Hoetjes. 1981. "The intrasponge fauna of *Spheciospongia vesparia* (Porifera, Demospongiae) at Curacao and Bonaire." *Marine Biology* 62:139–150.

26. Eibl-Eibesfeldt, I. 1975. Etiology–the biology of behavior. Holt, Rinehart and Winston, Inc. New York.

27. Kiene, W. 1988. "A model of bioerosion on the Great Barrier Reef." *Proceedings, 6th International Coral Reef Symposium* 3:449–454.

    Kiene, W., and P. A. Hutchings. 1994. "Bioerosion experiments on Lizard Island, Great Barrier Reef." *Coral Reefs* 13:91–98.

    Trudgill, S. T. 1983. "Measurements of rates of erosion of reefs and reef limestones." In: D. J. Barnes, ed. *Perspectives on Coral Reefs*. Brian Clouston Publishers, Manuka, ACT, Australia.

28. Wilkinson, Clive R. 1983. "Role of Sponges in Coral Reef Structural Processes." In: D. J. Barnes, ed. *Perspectives on Coral Reefs*. Brian Clouston Publishers (published for the Australian Institute of Marine Science).

29. Rutzler, K. 1975. "The role of burrowing sponges in bioerosion." *Oecologia* 19:203–216.

30. Goreau, T. F., and W. D. Hartman. 1966. "Sponge: effect on the form of reef corals." *Science* 151:343–344.

31. Hunter, Ian. 1977. "Sediment production by *Diadema antillarum* on a Barbados Reef." *Proceedings, 3d International Coral Reef Symposium* 2:106–109.

32. Ginsburg, R. N. 1983. "Geological and biological roles of cavities in coral reefs." In: D. J. Barnes, ed. *Perspectives on Coral Reefs*. Brian Clouston Publishers, Manuka, ACT, Australia.

33. Eakin, C. M. 1996. "Where have all the carbonates gone? A model comparison of calcium carbonate budgets before and after the 1982–1983 El Niño at Uva Island in the Eastern Pacific." *Coral Reefs* 15:109-119.

34. Grutter, A. S., and J. Hendrikz. 1999. "Diurnal variation in the abundance of juvenile parasitic gnathiid isopods on coral reef fish: implications for parasite-cleaner fish interactions." *Coral Reefs* 18:187–191.

35. Becker, J. H., and A.S. Grutter. 2004. "Cleaner shrimp do clean." *Coral Reefs* 23:515–520.

    Grutter, A. S. 1996. "Parasite removal rates by the cleaner wrasse *Labroides dimidiatus*." *Marine Ecology Progress Series* 130:61–70.

    Smit, N. J., and A. J. Davies. 1999. "New host records for *Haemogregarina bigemina* from the coast of southern Africa." *Journal of the Marine Biology Association of the United Kingdom* 79:933-935.

36. Paul, V. J., ed. 1992. *Explorations In Chemical Ecology: Ecological Roles of Marine Natural Products*. Cornell University Press, Ithaca, New York.

37. Chanas, B., and J. R. Pawlik. 1995. "Defense of Caribbean sponges against predatory reef fish. II. Spicules, tissue toughness and nutritional quality." *Marine Ecology Progress Series* 127:195–211.

Pawlik, J. R. et. al. 1995. "Defense of Caribbean sponges against predatory reef fish. I. Chemical deterrency." *Marine Ecology Progress Series* 127:183–194.

38. Pomponi, Shirley. 1999. "The bioprocess-technological potential of the sea." *Journal of Biotechnology* 70:5–13.

39. Faulkner, D. J. 1992. "Chemical defenses in marine molluscs." In: V. J. Paul, ed. *Ecological Roles of Marine Secondary Metabolites*. Cornell University Press, Ithaca, New York.

40. Buddemeier, R. W., and G. D. Fautin. 1993. "Coral bleaching as an adaptive mechanism." *BioScience* 43 (5):320–325.

    Gardner, T. A. et al. 2003. "Long-term region-wide declines in Caribbean corals." *Science*, 301:958–960.

    Glynn, P. W. 1990. "Coral mortality and disturbances to coral reefs in the tropical eastern Pacific." In: *Global Ecological Consequences of the 1982–83 El Niño-Southern Oscillation*. Elsevier Oceanography Series. Elsevier Press, Amsterdam.

    Hughes, T. P., and J. H. Connell. 1999. "Multiple stressors on coral reefs: A long-term perspective." *Limnology and Oceanography* 44(3, part 2):932–940.

    Pandolfi, J. B. C. 2005. "Enhanced: Are US Coral Reefs on the slippery slope to slime?" *Science*. 307:1725–1726.

41. Richardson, L. L. 1998. "Coral diseases: What is really known?" *Trends in Ecology and Evolution* 3:438–443.

42. Precht, W. F., and R. B. Aronson. 1997. "White-band disease in the Florida Keys—a continuing concern." *Reef Encounter* (Newsletter of the International Society for Reef Studies) 22:14–16.

43. Green, E. P. and A. W. Buckner, 2000. "The significance of coral disease epizootiology for coral reef conservation." *Biological Conservation* 96:347–361.

    Harvell, C. D., Kim, K., Burkholder, J. M., Colwell, R. R., Epstein, P. R., Grimes, D. J., Hofmann, E. E., Lipp, E. K., Osterhaus, A. D. M. E., Overstreet, R. M., Porter, J. W., Smith, G. W., and G. R. Vasta (1999). "Emerging marine diseases: Climate links and anthropogenic influence." *Science* 285:1505–1510.

    Porter J. W., Dunstan, P., Jaap, W. C., Patterson, L., Kosmynin, V., Meier, O. W., Patterson, M. E., and M. Par-

son (2001). "Patterns of spread of coral disease in the Florida keys." *Hydrobiologia* 460:1–24.

44. Buddemeier, R. W., and G. D. Fautin. 1993. "Coral Bleaching."

45. Hoegh-Guldberg, O. et al. 2000. "Pacific In Peril: Biological, Economic and Social Impacts of Climate Change on Pacific Coral Reefs." Special Report. Greenpeace International (www.greenpeace.org).

    Hughes, T. P. et al. 2003. "Climate change, human impacts, and the resilience of coral reefs." *Science* 301:929–933.

46. Brodie. J. et al. "Are increased nutrient inputs responsible for more outbreaks of crown-of-thorns starfish? An appraisal of the evidence." *Marine Pollution Bulletin* 512:266–278.

    Douglas, A.E. 2003. "Coral Bleaching—How and Why?" *Marine Pollution Bulletin* 46:385–392.

    Wilkinson, C. R., and R. W. Buddemeier. 1994. "Global Climate Change and Coral Reefs: Implications for People and Reefs." Report of the UNEP- IOC-ASPEI-IUCN Global Task Team on the Implications of Climate Change on Coral Reefs. IUCN, Gland, Switzerland.

47. Sapp, J. 1999. *What is Natural?: Coral Reef Crisis*. Oxford University Press. New York.

48. Hughes, T. P. 1994. "Catastrophes, phase shifts, and large-scale degradation of a Caribbean coral reef." *Science* 265:1547–1551.

49. Hughes, T. P. 1994. "Coral reef catastrophe." *Science* 266:1932–33.

50. Muscatine, L. et al. 1998. "Cell-specific density of symbiotic dinoflagellates in tropical anthozoans." *Coral Reefs* 17:329–337.

51. Ferrier-Pages, C. et al. 2000. "Effects of nutrient enrichment on growth and photosynthesis of the zooxanthellate coral *Stylophora pistillata*." *Coral Reefs*. 19:103-113.

    Hoegh-Guldberg, O. 2000. "The growth and survivorship of reef-building corals exposed to elevated temperatures and light in a long-term manipulation field study." Abstracts. 9th International Coral Reef Symposium. Bali, Indonesia.

    Klein, David. 2006. "Declining Caribbean Coral Reef

Communities: From Diverse Microbial Communities to Disease." Abstract. AAS Annual Meeting, February 2006.

52. Carriero-Silva, M. et al. 2005. "The role of inorganic nutrients in herbivory in controlling microbioerosion of carbonate substrate." *Coral Reefs*. 24:214–221.

Highsmith, R. C. 1980. "Geographic patterns of coral bioerosion: A Productivity hypothesis." *Journal of Experimental Marine Biology Ecology*. 46:177–196.

Hughes, T. P. 1994. "Coral Reef Catastrophe."

Rose, C. S., and M. J. Risk. 1985. "Increase in *Cliona delitrix* infestation of *Montastrea cavernosa* heads on an organically polluted portion of the Grand Cayman fringing reef." *Marine Ecology*. 6:345–363.

53. Shinn, E. A. and C. W. Holmes. 2000. "Coral reefs and the threat of soil dust." Abstract. 9th International Coral Reef Symposium. Bali, Indonesia.

54. Hayes, M. L. et al. 2000. "Dust to dust: Iron as the functional link between eolian dust and marine infectious diseases." Abstract. 9th International Coral Reef Symposium. Bali, Indonesia.

Ryan, J. C. 2001. "The Caribbean gets dusted." *BioScience* 51(5):334–338.

55. Hoegh-Guldberg, O. 2000. "The future of coral reefs: Integrating climate model projections and the recent behavior of corals and their dinoflagellates." Abstract. 9th International Coral Reef Symposium. Bali, Indonesia.

56. Pêcheux, M. 2000. "CO_2 rise is a main bleaching factor." Abstract. 9th International Coral Reef Symposium. Bali, Indonesia.

57. Lang, J. 1973. "Interspecific competition in Scleractinian corals. Why the race is not only to the swift." *Bulletin of Marine Science* 23:260–79.

Lang, J., and E. A. Chornesky. 1990. "Competition between Scleractinian reef corals—a review of mechanisms and effects." In: Z. Dubinsky, ed. *Ecosystems of the World*. Elsevier Publishing, New York.

58. Versluis, M. et al. 2000. "How Snapping Shrimp Snap: Through Cavitating Bubbles." *Science* 289:2020–21.

59. Halstead, B. 1988. *Poisonous and Venomous Marine Animals of the World* (2nd ed.). Darwin Press, Princeton, N.J.

60. Personal communication, Elan Corporation.

61. Hay, M. E. 1997. "The ecology and evolution of seaweed-herbivore interactions on coral reefs." *Coral Reefs* 16 (Supplement): s67–76.

62. Hay, M. E. et al. 1994. "Synergisms in plant defenses against herbivores: interactions of chemistry, calcification, and plant quality." *Ecology* 75: 1714–26.

63. Lobel, P. S. 1981. "Trophic biology of herbivorous reef fishes: alimentary pH and digestive capabilities." *Journal of Fisheries Biology* 19:365–97.

64. Hay, M. E. 1997. "The ecology and evolution of seaweed-herbivore interactions."

65. Gochfeld, D. J. 1996. "Chemical defense in the hard coral, *Porites compressa*." Abstract. 8th International Coral Reef Symposium. Panama.

66. Blinken, D. S. 2004. "Human Genome: End of the Beginning." *Nature* 431:915.

Claverie, Jean-Michel. 2000. "What if there are only 30,000 human genes?" *Science* 291(5507):1255–1257.

Lincoln D. S. "Human genome: End of the beginning." 2004. *Nature* 431:915–916.

67. Brenner, S. et al. 1993. "Characterization of the pufferfish (Fugu) genome as a compact model vertebrate genome." *Nature* 366(6452):265–268.

68. Halstead, B. 1988. *Poisonous and Venomous Marine Animals*.

69. Ormond, R. G. F. 1980. "Aggressive mimicry and other interspecific feeding associations among Red Sea coral reef predators." *Journal of Zoology Proceedings of the Zoological Society of London* 191:247–262.

70. Losey, G. 1971. "Communication between fishes in cleaning symbioses." In: T. C. Cheng, ed. *Aspects of the Biology of Symbioses*. Baltimore University Park Press, Maryland.

Ormond, R. G. F. 1980. "Aggressive mimicry."

71. Wickstein, M. K. 1995a. "Associations of fishes and their cleaners on coral reefs of Bonaire, Netherlands Antilles." *Copeia* 2:477–481.

Wickstein, M. K. 1995b. "Behavior of cleaners and their client fishes at Bonaire, Netherlands Antilles." *Journal of Natural History* 32:13–30.

72. Paul, V. J., ed. 1992. *Explorations in Chemical Ecology: Ecological Roles of Marine Natural Products*. Cornell University Press, Ithaca, New York.

73. Faulkner, D. John. 1992. "Chemical defenses in marine molluscs."

74. Ibid.

75. Lorenz, K. 1962. "The function of colour in coral reef fishes." *Proceedings of the Royal Institute of Great Britain* 39:282–296.

76. Losey, G. S. 1972. "Predation protection in the poison-fang blenny, *Meiacanthus atrodorsalis*, and its mimics, *Escenius bicolor* and *Runula laudadus* (Blennidae)." *Pacific Science* 26:129–139.

    Potts, G. W. 1973. "The ethology of *Labroides dimidiatus* (Cuv. & Val.) (Labridiae, Pices) on Aldabra." *Animal Behavior* 21:250–291.

    Randall, I. E., and H. A. Randall. 1960. "Examples of mimicry and protective resemblance in tropical marine fishes." *Bulletin of Marine Science of the Gulf and Caribbean* 10:444–480.

77. Grutter, A. et al. 2000. "Cheating in fish cleaning interactions." Abstract. 9th International Coral Reef Symposium. Bali, Indonesia.

78. Neudecker, S. 1989. "Eye camouflage and false eyespots: Chaetodontid responses to predators." *Environmental Biology of Fishes* 25:143–157.

79. Nemtzov, S. C. 1993. "Diel color phase changes in the coney, *Epinephelus fulvus* (Teleostie, Serranidae)." *Copeia* 3:883–885.

80. Grutter, S., and J. Hendrikz. 1999. "Diurnal variation in the abundance of juvenile parasitic gnathiid isopods on coral reef fish: Implications for parasite-cleaner fish interactions." *Coral Reefs* 18:187–191.

81. Van Rooij, J. M. et al. 1996. "The social and mating systems of the herbivorous reef fish *Sparisoma viride*: one-male versus multi-male groups." *Environmental Biology of Fishes* 47:353–378.

    Warner, R. R. 1984. "Mating systems and hermaphroditism in coral reef fish." *American Scientist* 72:128–136.

    Warner, R. R., and E. T. Schultz. 1992. "Sexual selection and male characteristics in the bluehead wrasse, *Thalassoma bifasciatum*, mating site acquisition, mating site defense, and female choice." *Evolution* 46:1421–1442.

82. Dawkins, R. 1989. *The Selfish Gene*. Oxford University Press, New York.

83. Godwin, J., and D. G. Fautin, 1992. "Defense of host actinians by anemonefishes." *Copeia* 3:908–902.

84. Ibid.

    Holbrook, S. J., and R.J. Schmitt. 2005. "Growth, Reproduction and survival of tropical sea anemone (Actinaria): Benefits of hosting anemone fish." *Coral Reefs* 24:67–73.

85. Ghiselin, M. T. 1969. "The evolution of hermaphroditism among animals." *Quarterly Review of Biology* 44:189–208.

    Thresher, R. E. 1984. *Reproduction in Reef Fishes*. T.G.H. Publications, Inc., New Jersey.

    Warner, R. R. 1991. "The use of phenotypic plasticity in coral reef fishes as test of theory in evolutionary ecology." In: P. Sale, ed. *The Ecology of Fishes on Coral Reefs*. Academic Press, New York.

86. Thresher, R. E. 1984. *Reproduction in Reef Fishes*.

87. Shapiro, D. Y. 1981. "The sequence of coloration changes during sex reversal in the tropical marine fish *Anthias squamipinnis* (Peters)." *Bulletin of Marine Science* 31:383–398.

    Shapiro, D. Y. 1981. "Size, maturation and the social control of sex reversal in the coral reef fish *Anthias squamipinnis*." *Journal of Zoology Proceedings of the Royal Society of London* 193:105–128.

88. Warner, R. R. and E. T. Schultz. 1992. "Sexual selection and male characteristics in the bluehead wrasse, *Thalassoma bifasciatum*, mating site acquisition, mating site defense, and female choice." *Evolution* 46:1421–1442.

89. Warner, R. R. et al. 1975. "Sex change and sexual selection." *Science* 190:633–638.

    Warner, R. R. 1975. "The adaptive significance of sequential hermaphoroditism in animals." *American Naturalist* 109:61-82.

90. Willis, B. L. et al. 1985. "Patterns in the mass spawning of corals on the Great Barrier Reef from 1981 to 1984." *Proceedings, 5th International Coral Reef Symposium* 4:343–340, Tahiti.

91. Birkeland, C. 1997. *Life and Death of Coral Reefs*. University of Guam.

    Carr, M. H., T. W. Anderson, and M. A. Hixon. 2002. Biodiversity, population regulation, and the stability of coral-reef fish communities. *Proceedings of the Natural Academy of Sciences* 99(17): 11241–11245.

Grigg, R. W. 2000. "Coral reef evolution: short term instability versus Evolutionary stasis." *Integrated Coastal Zone Management*.

Hixon, M. A., and W. N. Brostoff. 1996. "Succession and herbivory: Effects of differential fish grazing on Hawaiian coral-reef algae." *Ecological Monographs* 66:67–90.

Jackson, et al. 2001. "Historical overfishing and the recent collapse of coastal ecosystems." *Science* 293:629–638.

Karlson, R. H. 1999. *Dynamics of Coral Communities*. Kluwer Academic Publishers. Boston.

Sammarco, P. W. 1980. "Diadema and its relationship to coral spat mortality: Grazing, competition, and biological disturbances." *Journal of Experimental Marine Biology and Ecology* 45: 245–272.

92. Hay, M. E. 1984. "Patterns of fish and urchin grazing on Caribbean coral reefs: Are previous results typical?" *Ecology* 65:446–454.

Hughes, T. P. 1994. "Catastrophes, phase shifts, and large-scale degradation of a Caribbean coral reef." *Science* 265:1547–51.

Littler, M. M. et al. 2006. "Harmful algae on tropical coral reefs: bottom -up eutrophication and top-down herbivory." In press.

93. Bellwood, D. R., and T. P. Hughes. 2000. "Regional-Scale Assembly Rules and Biodiversity of Coral Reefs." *Science* 292(5521):1532–1535.

Hoegh-Guldberg, O., et al. 2000. "Pacific In Peril."

Wilkinson, C. R., and R. W. Buddemeier. 1994. "Global Climate Change and Coral Reefs."

94. Connell, J. H. 1978. "Diversity in Tropical Rainforests and Coral Reefs." *Science* 199(4335):1302–1310.

95. Connell, J. H. 1997. "Disturbance and recovery of coral assemblages." *Coral Reefs* 16 (Supplement):s101–113.

Cornell, H. V., and R. H. Karlson. 2000. "Coral species richness: Ecological Versus biogeographical influences." *Coral Reefs* 19:37–49.

LIST OF ILLUSTRATIONS

PLATES

FIGURES

INDEX

173